APPLIQUÉ
with
Folded Cutwork

Anita Shackelford

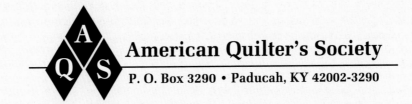

American Quilter's Society

P. O. Box 3290 • Paducah, KY 42002-3290

Located in Paducah, Kentucky, the American Quilter's Society (AQS) is dedicated to promoting the accomplishments of today's quilters. Through its publications and events, AQS strives to honor today's quiltmakers and their work and to inspire future creativity and innovation in quiltmaking.

EDITOR: BONNIE K. BROWNING

TECHNICAL EDITOR: BARBARA SMITH

BOOK DESIGN/ILLUSTRATIONS: CASSIE ENGLISH

COVER DESIGN: MICHAEL BUCKINGHAM

PHOTOGRAPHY: CHARLES R. LYNCH, UNLESS OTHERWISE NOTED

AUTHOR'S PHOTO BY JIM CARROLL

Library of Congress Cataloging-in-Publication Data

Shackelford, Anita

    Appliqué with folded cutwork / by Anita Shackelford

                p.   cm.

    Includes bibliographical references (p. 142-43).

    ISBN 1-57432-723-2

    1. Appliqué. 2. Appliqué--Patterns.   I. Title.

TT779.S42   1999

746.44'5041--dc21   98-32283

                                              CIP

Additional copies of this book may be ordered from the American Quilter's Society, PO Box 3290, Paducah, KY 42002-3290 @ $22.95. Add $2.00 for postage and handling.

Printed in the U.S.A. by Image Graphics, Paducah, KY

ACKNOWLEDGMENTS

With each book I have written, the circle of friendship has grown larger. Many people have contributed their time and talents to this project and to each, I say thank you!

To my family for understanding my obsession and giving me the time to work and to share my love of quilts with others and especially to my husband, Richard, for his unfailing love and support and for enjoying the journey with me.

To the Kidron Community Historical Society, Kidron, Ohio; New England Quilt Museum, Lowell, Massachusetts; and Union County Historical Society, Lewisburg, Pennsylvania, for sharing quilts from their collections.

To Cindy Cimo, Xenia Cord, Ruth Erickson, Carolyn Guest, Kurt and Ellen Heck, Erica Jarrett, Suzanne Karl, Theodore Karl, Ruth Kennedy, Sheila Kennedy, Jo Lischynski, Susan Nicholson, Emily Senuta, Connie St. Clair, Noel W. Tenney, and Marilyn Woodin for sharing works of their own hands or other special pieces.

To a special group of friends: Glenda Clark, Janet Hamilton, Ruth Kennedy, Sheila Kennedy, Jo Lischynski, Connie St. Clair, and Rebecca Whetstone for sharing their talents and keeping me inspired.

To Bill and Meredith Schroeder and American Quilter's Society for giving me the opportunity to share my work with others in so many ways.

To my editor and friend, Bonnie K. Browning, and executive editor, Barbara Smith, for helping to make this idea become a reality.

To photographer Charles R. Lynch for capturing the beauty of the quilts.

To designers Cassie English for the layout and Michael Buckingham for the cover.

CONTENTS

INTRODUCTION

For many years, I have been fascinated with the process of folding paper to cut symmetrical designs. I have been drawn to antique red and green quilts with simple, stylized appliqué. It is easy to see that many of these patterns were made by cutting the design from a folded piece of paper. I have used the paper cutting technique many times to create simple leaf and floral shapes for my own appliqué quilts.

This book represents a long period of study into the variety of designs that can be created by cutting paper which has been folded to produce simple mirror images or multiple repeats. The look of this work is quite different from the dimensional appliqué style, which I love. Although these cutwork designs are flat and have much simpler lines, they are very exciting. The design process is perhaps the most fun; cutting and recutting, never knowing for sure how the design will look until it is unfolded. Usually, I am pleasantly surprised.

The human eye finds something very satisfying in symmetry and the balance of repeated images. Even the simplest or most mundane shapes become beautiful when they are mirrored or repeated. The type of pattern created with this technique depends on how the paper is folded, how much of the paper is used, and the complexity of the design. Learning where to place major and minor motifs on the folded paper will enable you to create the designs that you want.

The Study of Design Styles section explains in detail the paper-folding technique and pattern design. The process is presented in simple to complex progression. Design styles included in the book run the full gamut from the simple folk art shapes of traditional New England samplers and Baltimore album quilts to elaborate Pennsylvania German scherenschnitte and Polynesian florals. In addition to the simple symmetry of hearts and folk art flowers, there are instructions to help you create spectacular radiating designs which repeat four, five, six, eight, or ten times. Long borders can also be designed with this technique, if the paper is folded and cut paper-doll style. As you read through the explanations of the individual styles, try cutting a small sample of each. More than one hundred patterns are provided, but learning to cut your own designs is exciting and will give you a quilt that is uniquely yours.

Choosing fabrics to set a mood, overall layout of blocks, and other design considerations are covered in the Getting Started section. The Techniques section includes close-up, step-by-step photos of needle-turn appliqué. It is an exciting opportunity for me to be able to show the fine points of appliqué hands-on in much the same way that I demonstrate it in a classroom setting. Other appliqué techniques covered are cut-away appliqué, reverse appliqué, blind stitch by machine, and finishing edges with decorative stitches. Beyond appliqué, the designs can also be translated into fabric in other ways, such as stencil painting, silk screen printing, or quilting.

Cutting your own designs will give you the freedom to make a quilt in any size and style your heart desires. Try your hand at paper cutting and discover an exciting way to create your next quilt.

Appliqué with Folded Cutwork: Anita Shackelford

1 HISTORY OF CUTWORK
part one

HISTORY OF CUTWORK

The art of folded cutwork may be as old as paper and scissors themselves. The history of papercutting is well documented in China during the first century A.D. Decorative paper cuttings, called window flowers, were hung in windows while paper cuttings placed on doors served as both decorative and protective images.

When the Spanish arrived in Central America, they found the native Otomi people using a folded technique to cut symmetrical images from a type of paper made from tree bark. These figures or gods were used by the shaman in religious and other social ceremonies. Today, tissue paper designs, called *papel picado* or pierced paper, are often used as decorations during holidays and other celebrations.

The technique of cutting pictures from paper spread through most of eastern Europe during the sixteenth and seventeenth centuries. This time-consuming work was respected as art and was popular with the educated classes. *Scherenschnitte* was usually made with black cutwork laid on top of white paper or in reverse, with white on top of black, to produce a very strong value contrast. Even the finest of details could be clearly reproduced. Flora, fauna, animal, and human figures were often used in combination to create delicate and elaborate pictures (1-1).

1-1. LINDEN TREE HOSTESS demonstrates the extremely intricate detail of a traditional *scherenschnitte* design. 7" x 8" single layer, asymmetrical design cut from black paper and laid onto white background. Early twentieth century, Germany. Courtesy of Kurt and Ellen Heck, Somis, California.

These designs might be cut from a single flat sheet of paper for asymmetrical shapes, or from folded paper which produced repeated images (1-2). Cut paper designs were used for valentines (1-3), gifts for friends, and tokens for weddings and other special events. In their more permanent form, these designs were framed for hanging on the wall, or mounted in keepsake albums.

Quilt historians agree that these cutwork paper shapes provided the inspiration for a similar style of design which was used in mid-nineteenth century appliqué quilts. Appliquéd cutwork began to be included in album quilts in the 1830s and early 1840s at the same time that quilt design changed from the medallion arrangement to the block format. Historian Jennifer Goldsborough found in her research that the earliest Baltimore album quilts combined red and green cutwork squares with floral designs cut from calico and chintz fabrics. Quiltmakers living in cities, or those with close ties to other quiltmakers, often shared patterns. The simple fleur-de-lis appears to have been the most common cutwork design used in early Maryland friendship quilts (1-4).

1-3. Multiple-fold fraktur friendship token, 1886 from Steiner family. 14" diameter. Collection of Kidron Community Historical Society, Kidron, Ohio.

1-2. Single fold tree of life (*leluje*) design. 3" x 5", cut with 13" sheep shears in the traditional *leluje* style of the Kurpie region of northeastern Poland. Cut by Carolyn E. Guest, East St. Johnsbury, Vermont, 1998.

1-4. FLEUR-DE-LIS, a typical design in Maryland friendship quilts, stitched by the author.

CUMBERLAND COUNTY QUILT

1-5. CUMBERLAND COUNTY QUILT, 70¾" x 70¾". Four-block appliquéd cutwork of red and green printed calico on white, made in Cumberland County, Pennsylvania. The quilt is bordered with continuous cutwork designs which are butted into border seams. Quilted with grid background and running feathers, nine stitches per inch. Collection of Wilma Harlacher DeVanney. Photo courtesy of Union County Historical Society, Lewisburg, Pennsylvania.

German quiltmakers in Pennsylvania and surrounding areas translated both simple and elaborate scherenschnitte designs into appliquéd quilts, which were made in bold colors including combinations of red, green, and orange (1-5).

Quiltmakers in more isolated areas often had to depend on their own talents or inspiration and materials at hand to create patterns for appliqué. Interesting stories about patterns cut or torn by itinerant peddlers have been documented several times. In her 1949 *American Quilts and Coverlets*, Florence Peto made reference to a peddler cutting a paper pattern for a quiltmaker in Lancaster, Pennsylvania. Similar stories are told in *Quilts of Tennessee* of three peddler quilts made between 1855 and 1870. The current documentation project in West Virginia includes a story of a pattern torn from a piece of newspaper by a Polish lumber camp worker. This quilt was appliquéd by three young sisters at the turn of the century (1-6).

Many people associate the fold-and-cut style of appliqué with Hawaiian quilts. The history of these quilts probably began when a group of missionaries and their wives arrived in Hawaii from New England in the early nineteenth century. Hawaiian women and children were taught the art of paper cutting along with sewing and quiltmaking. It seems natural that the beautiful surroundings influenced the imagery of their cutwork designs. Traditional Hawaiian appliqué is cut from one large piece of fabric for a whole cloth look rather than the small blocks used in the album style (1-7, p. 12).

Ireland and Wales also have a history of appliquéd cutwork with a slightly different style. These quilts include many cutwork shapes appliquéd onto a whole cloth background, arranged in either a medallion or a block-style format.

1-6. Appliqué quilt with complex Polish *wycinanki* paper cut design, made c. 1890 by Arzeltha May Osburn (Mills) and her two sisters in southern Upshur County, West Virginia. Appliquéd with a blanket stitch. Background quilting in outline, cross hatch, and feathers. Collection of Noel W. Tenney, Tallmansville, West Virginia. Photo courtesy of West Virginia Heritage Quilt Search and Jurgen Lorenzen, photographer.

PAPER CUTTING IN MANY LANGUAGES

CHINESE	chien-chih	(jian-jeh)
JAPANESE	monkiri	(mon-kee-ree)
GERMAN	scherenschnitte	(sher-en-shnit-uh)
SWISS	scherenschnitte	(sher-en-shnit-uh)
POLISH	wycinanki	(vee-chee-non-kee)
DUTCH	knippen	(knip-pen)
ENGLISH	papercutting	

BLUE HAWAIIAN

1-7. BLUE HAWAIIAN. Traditional Hawaiian quilt features an elaborate center medallion and full border cut from one piece of blue cloth, appliquéd onto a white background. Maker unknown, c. 1920. The echo quilting that surrounds the design is called *Kuiki lau* in Hawaiian. Photo courtesy of New England Quilt Museum, Lowell, Massachusetts. Gift of Gail Binney-Stiles.

2 STUDY OF DESIGN STYLES

part two

STUDY OF DESIGN STYLES

I n my workshops on paper folding for appliqué patterns, the students begin by cutting samples from small pieces of scrap paper to get a feel for the process. I find that most beginners are also more comfortable with the design process if shapes are first drawn onto the paper. The motifs can be evaluated and changed, if necessary, before they are cut.

Probably the first and most important way to be successful with cutwork appliqué is to cut designs which match your own skill level. Smooth lines and gentle curves will be much quicker to cut and easier to appliqué. Motifs that include very narrow stems, complex lines, and sharp points will require more skill. Keep in mind that the number of elements and the amount of detail in the finished block will be repeated up to eight times. Read through the design section of the book and cut samples of the various styles to see how each one is formed. Find out which ones you like. You may discover that you have your own style. For now, don't worry if the patterns are the wrong size or are not perfect shapes. Some will be good, some can be modified, and some will go directly into the waste basket. The more designs you cut, the easier the process becomes. Working on a small scale makes it easier to see the proportions or to make corrections, and small shapes are easier to cut. Relax and have fun. Remember, this is only paper!

2-1. FOLK ART SAMPLER, 18" x 24", by the author, 1997. Folk art shapes all made with the simple symmetry technique. Hand-dyed cottons on wool; edges blanket stitched with crewel wool.

SIMPLE SYMMETRY

For simple symmetry, the paper is folded only once. The fold is vertical and the cut begins and ends on the folded edge (2-2). A pattern cut on a single fold produces a design with symmetrical halves (mirror images).

Folk Art

An amazing variety of images can be produced with simple symmetry. A heart shape is an obvious choice. Everyone has cut this simple shape from a folded piece of paper. When the design is drawn, the beginning and the end of the line must touch the fold so that, when it is cut, the motif will stay together and the background will fall away. To try a simple symmetrical shape, fold a small piece of paper in half. Cut half of a heart shape through both layers of paper and unfold it to see your symmetrical template (2-3). Now, try your hand at some others, such as a tulip, leaf, pineapple, basket, apple, gingerbread man, or tree (2-4). Keep in mind that, for a smooth shape across a fold, the line must cross perpendicular (at a right angle) to the fold. For example, with a gingerbread man, if the line that forms the top of the head is slanted or curved to the inside, a dented shape will be formed. If the line is slanted or curved to the outside, the result will be a pointed head shape (2-5).

All of the appliqué templates for the FOLK ART SAMPLER in 2-1 were made with the simple symmetry technique.

2-3. Cutting line begins and ends on the fold.

2-4. Any symmetrical shape can be cut on a single fold.

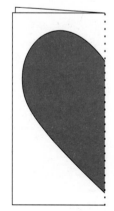

2-2. Half of a heart shape positioned on the fold.

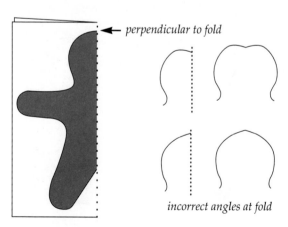

perpendicular to fold

incorrect angles at fold

2-5. For a smooth head shape, the cutting line must go straight across the fold.

Silhouettes

Silhouettes are another familiar shape that can be cut from paper. These paper "shadows" were a favorite art form of M. Etienne De Silouette, French minister of finance in the mid-eighteenth century, and the technique bears his name. Simple silhouettes are easy to trace and fun to cut. When a silhouette shape is positioned "face to face," interesting things happen in the negative space. A silhouette vase is a clever way to include yourself in a quilt or to personalize it for a family member or friend. Begin by tracing a silhouette of your loved one (2-6). Place the drawing on a folded piece of paper, facing toward, but positioned slightly away from the fold. Try several variations with the silhouette close to the fold, farther apart, or at an angle. Copy the silhouette and then add lines to form the top and the base of the container. Be sure that these lines extend over the fold so that the motif will be complete. Cut out the design through both layers of paper and unfold it to reveal your personalized vase. Figure 2-7 shows how I used my own silhouette to personalize a tall, thin vase.

While the shape of the vase shown in 2-8 is more complex than the simpler designs, its pattern was also created with a cut which began and ended on a single center fold.

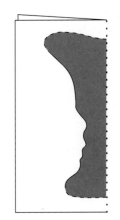

2-6. Simple symmetry vases and variations using a silhouette.

2-7. Silhouette vase from LONE STAR WITH BRODERIE PERSE, made by the author, 1994.

2-8. Elaborate, unusual vase shape created using the simple symmetry technique. Made by the author, 1997.

Appliqué with Folded Cutwork: Anita Shackelford

Filigree Designs

It is possible to create designs that are much more complex in appearance but are still based on a single fold. These complex filigree designs are made with a single cut for the outline of the design and include many areas of reverse appliqué for interior detailing. A wall quilt, HEARTS AFIRE!, uses the technique of filigree cutwork and reverse appliqué to create a complex heart design (2-9). Instructions for reverse appliqué are on page 73.

Designs with a Center Motif

When half of a design is cut on the fold and an asymmetrical motif is placed beside it (2-10), a symmetrical design with a center focus is created. The center will feature a single motif, while a full design will repeat on each side, facing toward or away from the center. These designs may be planned to fill a square or may be lengthened to fill a horizontal or vertical space. The block in 2-10 features a simple vase combined with flowers and a pair of birds. The vase was cut on the fold in a simple symmetry design, while the triple flowers and the birds show the more complex arrangement of a design with a center motif.

An appliquéd cutwork pillow sham shown in (2-11, p.18) features a beautiful design of deer in the woods. The scene was made more complex and visually pleasing by cutting the shape through two layers to form a symmetrical image.

2-10. The vase with birds block was cut using the technique of a design with a center motif.

2-9. HEARTS AFIRE! by the author, 1997. Areas of reverse appliqué were used to create a filigree design within a simple symmetrical heart.

A

2-11.
A. Deer pattern, placing half of a tree on the fold and a full deer shape beside it, creates a symmetrical design with a center motif.
B. DEER IN THE WOODS pillow sham, from the collection of Erica Jarrett, Libertyville, Illinois.

PAPER FOLDING FOR MULTIPLE REPEATS

The majority of cutwork appliqué designs are based on four or eight repeats within the block. With this technique, the designs are uniform and symmetrical because all the motifs are cut at one time through all of the layers of paper, creating the more familiar snowflake patterns. The patterns may be made in any size or style, but they have one thing in common. The paper will be folded into eighths for most of these design styles.

It is important to learn the proper fold to prepare the paper for cutting patterns with multiple repeats. Study the directions carefully to make sure you are using the right fold for the design. Expect that, even after many successful designs, an occasional pattern may still be cut incorrectly and fall apart. It happens even to experienced papercutters.

Begin by folding a square of paper in half, (2-12A) and in half again in the opposite direction (2-12B). Look carefully at the edges and corners. One corner will be completely open (raw edges if this were fabric) and the opposite corner will be completely closed. The closed corner is the center of the paper. Draw a line, real or imaginary, radiating from the closed corner to the open corner (2-12C). This line represents the placement of the final folds.

All the layers of paper could be folded, one more time along this line, to produce the necessary one-eighth design space. However, you will find that the folds will be less bulky and your cut will be more accurate if half the paper is folded to the front (2-12D) and half is folded to the back (2-12E) to form a butterfly shape (2-12F). To see if you have done this correctly, unfold the paper and check the fold lines. They should all cross in the center (2-13). If your paper is folded with a plus sign (+) and a square on point (2-14), the last folds were made in the wrong direction and the paper will fall apart when the pattern is cut.

After you are certain that the paper has been folded correctly, compare it to 2-15 to identify several important areas. The center of the paper will have no open edges. There will be one long fold and one short fold, which also have no open edges. The third side will be all open. If you have any variations, recheck the folds.

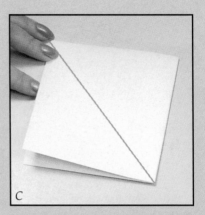

2-12.
A. Fold paper in half; *B.* fold in half again in the opposite direction; *C.* line radiating from center of paper to open corner shows position of fold; *D.* fold top layer to front; *E.* fold bottom layer to the back; *F.* paper should be folded into a butterfly shape.

2-13. Open paper to check folds; all fold lines should cross in center.

2-14. Square on point indicates incorrect fold.

2-15. Paper folded into eighths with center point, long fold, and short fold for design placement.

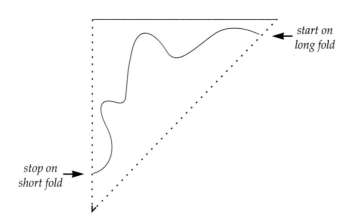

2-16. Four corners design.

start on long fold

stop on short fold

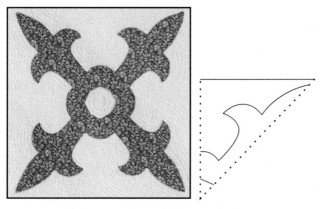

2-17. Narrow Fleur-de-lis motifs fills only part of background block.

Four Corners

The simplest shape to cut from a one-eighth fold is one that has four symmetrical motifs extending into the four corners of the background block. The cut for a four corners design begins near the outside or open end of the long fold and ends near the center of the paper on the short fold (2-16). For the pattern to remain in one piece, the cut must begin on one fold and end on the other fold. Four corners designs may be delicate (2-17) or bold (2-18), depending upon how much of the paper is used when the design is cut. Making full use of the paper produces a design that fills the background space, while a narrower pattern will fill only the corners.

Four Plus Four

The next step in making a more complex pattern is to cut motifs along both the long and the short folds. The addition of a motif on the short fold will produce a design with four main elements and four secondary motifs. To create a four plus four design, fold the paper into eighths as before. Begin the cut near the outside or open end of the long fold, cut in toward the center and finish somewhere on the short fold (2-19).

A four plus four design can include one long and one short motif (2-20), one heavy and one delicate motif (2-21), or one large and one small motif (2-22), depending on how much of the short fold is used.

2-18. *A*. Larger coxcomb motif fills block more completely; *B*. COXCOMB, large four block, made by the author, 1986. This is the author's first quilt using the folded cutwork technique. Coxcomb pattern by Gwen Marston.

Appliqué with Folded Cutwork: Anita Shackelford

FOUR PLUS FOUR

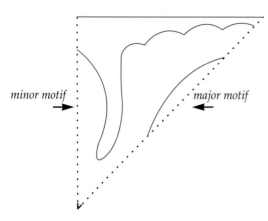

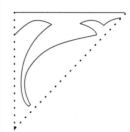

2-21. Heavy and delicate motifs in Pineapple and Leaves.

2-19. Major motif cut from the long fold and minor motif cut from the short fold creates a four plus four design.

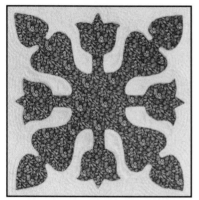

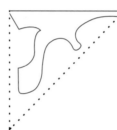

2-20. Long and short motifs of similar weight in Hearts and Tulips.

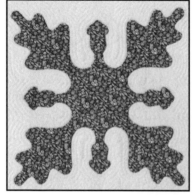

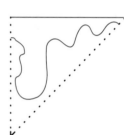

2-22. Large and small motifs in Oak Leaves and Acorns

Four Plus Eight

A four plus eight pattern will be created when half of the main design is cut on the long fold, and a full minor motif is cut from the body of the paper near the short fold. The minor motif may be symmetrical or asymmetrical, as desired. Each pattern will produce a balanced design when repeated in the block. The paper should be folded in a one-eighth fold. A good example of a four plus eight design is a flower and a pair of leaves. A good example of a four plus eight design. Begin the cut for the flower or the major motif near the outside edge of the long fold. Bring the cut line in toward the center. Rather than ending with a motif positioned on the short fold, cut a full leaf or minor design element within the remaining paper. End the cutting line near the center of the short fold (2-23).

FOUR PLUS EIGHT

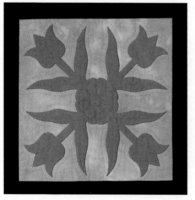

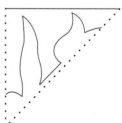

2-23. Full leaf design cut in body of folded paper in Tulips and Leaves.

EIGHT ALL AROUND

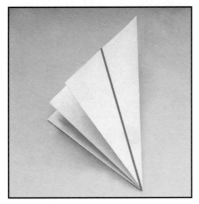

2-24. Additional fold to find center line for eight all around designs.

EVEN EIGHT

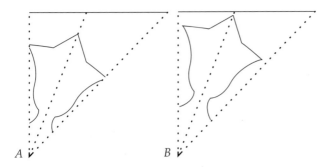

2-25. Even eight
A. Motif connected at center and across both folds; B. motif connected at center only.

2-26. Simple symmetry tulip produces an even eight design.

Eight All Around

Paper folded into eighths also offers the possibility of a design with eight balanced repeats. To prepare a design space for eight all around, fold the paper into eighths, and then fold the top layer one more time to create a center line in this space (2-24). Unfold the top layer and use the center fold line to position a motif that will repeat eight times. Both symmetrical and asymmetrical motifs should be centered on this line. The cut for an eight all around design begins near the center on one fold and ends near the center on the other fold. The pattern may also be connected by extending the design across the folds at another position, depending on the shape of the motif.

Even eight

A symmetrical motif placed in the center of the design space will produce an even eight pattern. To begin, use the simple symmetry technique as described on page 15 to create a simple symmetrical pattern. This small pattern must fit within a 45° triangle. Center the pattern on the folded paper and trace the design (2-25). The cut for an even eight design should begin on one fold and end on the other fold, the same distance from the center. Cutting this symmetrical shape in the center of all eight layers of paper will produce eight identical and evenly spaced motifs (2-26).

Asymmetrical eight

An asymmetrical motif will produce a design that repeats all around, but faces toward and away from itself. This works well when making a pattern from hands, which naturally come in pairs (2-27). You might also use flags or palm trees swaying in the breeze.

Twinning will occur when an even eight motif is not centered on the paper. If the motif is cut closer to one fold than the other, the unfolded pattern will show pairs of motifs that are positioned close together rather than individual motifs which are evenly spaced (2-28).

Another fun idea for an asymmetrical eight is to write your name or a message in the one-eighth space (2-29). Interesting patterns develop when letters are mirrored and repeated around a design. The design can be positioned lengthwise along the center fold of the paper, or it can travel from the long to the short fold, but it must touch both sides at some point. Ruth Erickson of Terre Haute, Indiana, used this technique to add her granddaughter's name to a block in the album quilt Ruth is making for her. To Ruth's surprise and delight, the letter "J" formed a heart shape when it was repeated across the fold.

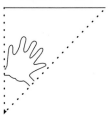

2-27. Baby hands produce motifs that face toward and away from each other.

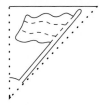

2-28. Positioning a single motif off-center will create twin motifs.

2-29. Letters, JEN, used to create an interesting asymmetrical eight design.

Six-Sided

As a variation on eight all around, paper can be folded into six even layers to produce a hexagonal or six-sided design. Begin, as before, by folding the paper in half (2-30*A*, p. 24). Fold it in half the other direction and pinch it at the fold to mark the center (2-30*B*). Measure 60° from the fold and mark a line radiating from the center point to the 60° mark (2-30*C*). Folding from the center point, bring the opposite folded edge up to match this line (2-30*D*). Fold the third layer to the back (2-30*E*) to create three even wedges, with a Z-shaped fold (2-30*F*). The folds will be more uniform if one layer is folded to the front and one to the back. The outside edges of the paper will not be even, as they were in the one-eighth fold, but this will not affect the pattern. With a little practice, you will be able to make this Z-fold by eye. You may want to open the paper to check the folds before you cut the design; all the fold lines should cross in the center.

Symmetrical or asymmetrical motifs can be used in six-sided designs and should be centered on the paper as in eight all around. The motif must be a shape to fit within a 60° triangle. This may be the place to use a motif that was too large to fit into a one-eighth fold. Any design will be effective repeated six times, but this shape is, of course, perfect for a snowflake (2-31, p. 24).

Five-Pointed

A square piece of paper can also be folded to create a design with five even repeats. It is surprising to see a cutwork design with only five repeats, such as the palm-tree block (2-32), but any motif can be made to repeat five times. Five points are perfect for simple star shapes, and they can also be the beginning of a number of variations.

SIX-SIDED FOLDING

2-30.
A. Fold paper in half; B. fold in half in the opposite direction and pinch to mark the center; C. mark line at 60° angle; D. bring folded edge up to match line; E. fold remaining layer to back; F. Z-shaped fold.

Fig. 2-31. A six-sided fold is used for a snowflake design.

2-32. Antique block shows a palm tree motif repeated five times. Palm trees from SNOWFLAKE, collection of Marilyn Woodin (quilt shown on p. 66).

To create the necessary folds for five repeats, begin by folding a square piece of paper in half (2-33A). Measure ⅓ of the distance down from the open corner on one side. Bring the opposite bottom corner up to match this point and crease the fold (2-33B). Fold this newly made edge over again to match the first line and crease (2-33C). Fold the remaining original layers behind to make the final fold (2-33D). As with the other styles, all fold lines should cross in the center (2-33E). The outside edges of the paper will be uneven with this

Appliqué with Folded Cutwork: Anita Shackelford

type of fold. Be sure that the design does not extend beyond the shortest fold on either side.

A five-pointed star can be created by cutting half of a star from fold to fold. The sharper the angle on this cut, the sharper the star point will be (2-34*A*, p. 26). A more delicate cutwork design can be created by cutting reverse appliqué areas from the fold (2-34*B*). Any other design that repeats five times can also be cut from this five-pointed star fold by using the four corners method, although most often five repeats do not fill a square block adequately. Even at its fullest, a five-pointed star cut from an 8" square of paper will be 8" across, but only 7¾" tall and may appear to be smaller than other design styles cut from the same size paper.

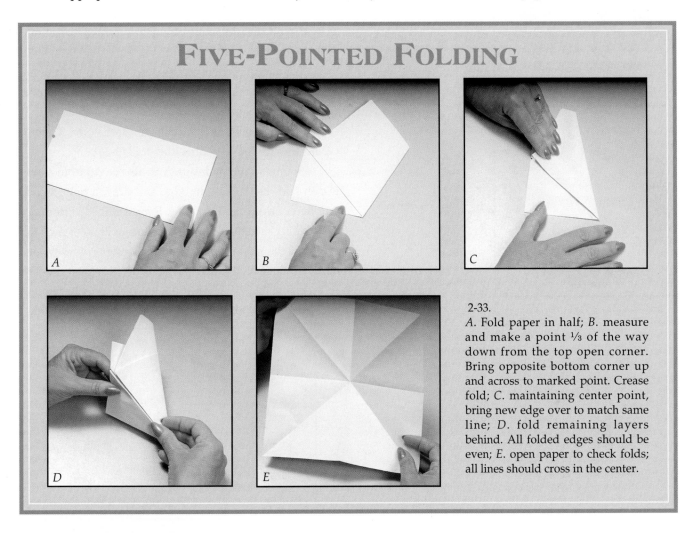

FIVE-POINTED FOLDING

2-33.
A. Fold paper in half; *B.* measure and make a point ⅓ of the way down from the top open corner. Bring opposite bottom corner up and across to marked point. Crease fold; *C.* maintaining center point, bring new edge over to match same line; *D.* fold remaining layers behind. All folded edges should be even; *E.* open paper to check folds; all lines should cross in the center.

FIVE-POINTED

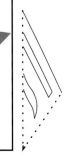

2-34. *A.* A single cut creates a five-pointed star; *B.* areas of reverse appliqué create a filigree design.

C

D

2-34. *C.* Cutting points from both folds creates a ten-pointed star. *D.* a simple symmetry design centered on the paper creates a design with ten repeats.

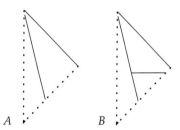

A   B

2-35. *A.* A single line on the long fold will create four compass points. *B.* adding a line on the short fold creates a square and compass.

2-36. Adding a center shape adds interest to a compass design.

Ten-Pointed

Cutting a point from both folds of the five-fold paper creates a ten-pointed star (2-34*C*) or using the eight all around method will create a ten-repeat design (2-34*D*). These designs are more nearly circular and will fill a square block more uniformly than a design with only five points.

Angular Designs
Compass, Star, Sunburst

For a traditional compass design, begin by drawing a point on the long fold (2-35*A*). This one line will produce the north, south, east, and west points. Other shapes may be added behind the basic compass points (2-35*B*). Open areas can be cut from either fold (2-36).

Star or sunburst designs can also be cut from a one-eighth fold. Use a straight edge and draw a point which will be cut from the long fold. Repeat this idea to add a point along the short fold. These lines will meet near the center of the paper. For a sunburst design, more points, either straight or curved, can be added between the two major points (2-37*A,B*). Fold the top layer of paper in half to find the center placement for these additional points.

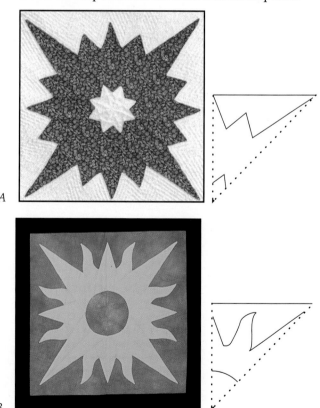

A

B

2-37. *A.* Additional points can be added on the short fold and in between the long and short folds for more complex star designs; *B.* adding curved lines changes points to flames in this sunburst pattern.

Scherenschnitte

Paper cutting is called "scherenschnitte" in German and "wycinanki" in Polish. Although these terms include all styles of paper cutting, this section will focus on the open, lacy, repeated images that are referred to as stars or snowflakes. Early cut paper designs often used a combination of techniques including symmetrical cutting, layering of several colors, collage, painting, and pin pricking. Inscribed cutwork papers were also, on occasion, given as love tokens, or what we might think of as valentines. The most complex of these designs are folded and cut so that their patterns repeat 8, 16, or even 32 times. These designs can be extremely intricate when cut from paper, since the edges are not turned (2-38).

Working in fabric may limit the complexity of multiple-fold scherenschnitte designs, but a similar look can still be obtained. This type of cut paper design is characterized by a shaped outside edge and intricate areas of reverse appliqué (see page 73 for reverse appliqué technique). The outside edges of the pattern can be cut to produce several basic shapes, such as round or star-shaped designs. Small cut-outs added along the folds will produce areas of reverse appliqué within the motif for the traditional lace-like appearance. 2-39A shows a simple appliqué cut in the scherenschnitte style. The outside edge has been cut with a gentle S curve. Arcs and hearts have been cut from the folds.

Unless noted, scherenschnitte designs in squares, circles, snowflakes, and stars begin with the paper folded into eighths.

2-38. Gwiazda, 8" star papercut mounted on a 12" square. Cut by Carolyn E. Guest, East St. Johnsbury, Vermont, 1998.

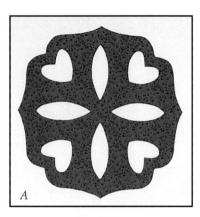

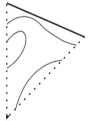

2-39. *A.* A shaped outer edge and areas of reverse appliqué create a simple scherenschnitte design.

B

2-39. *B*. Square-shaped scherenschnitte design.

A

B

2-40 *A, B*. Circular-shaped scherenschnitte design.

A

B   C

Square

For an appliqué motif that is to remain square, begin by adding a pleasing shape to the outside open edge. Consider a gently curved shape, repeating scallops, or sharp points (2-39*B*). Cut-out shapes should be added on both the long and the short folds. These are isolated cuts that begin and end on the same fold to produce the small open areas for reverse appliqué. Traditional shapes might include hearts, diamonds, circles, ovals, or arcs. Don't worry if the small shapes do not appear to work together. Repetition and symmetry will create a pleasing balance in the finished piece.

Circle

If the appliqué is to have a circular shape, use a compass to scribe a true arc along the open edge of the folded paper. Set the point of the compass at the center of the folded paper and the pencil at the outer edge of the short fold and draw the cutting line. Cut the curved outer edge along this line and then add cut-outs on both folds (2-40) as with the square.

Snowflake

A snowflake shape can be cut from a folded square of paper or from a folded circle. Cut from a square, the snowflake will have long and short crystals and will extend into the corners of the block (2-41*A*). Cut from a circle, the crystals will all be the same length and will fill the center of the background block in the same manner as a circular design (2-41*B*). Begin a snowflake by cutting the reverse appliqué shapes from both folds. Finally, cut into the body of the paper, echoing the shape of the cut-outs to separate the long crystals from each other (2-41*C*). A fold for a six-sided design will create a more realistic snowflake.

2-41. *A*. Snowflake-style scherenschnitte cut from a square will have long and short crystals; *B*. snowflake-style schereschnitte cut from a circle will have crystals all the same length; *C*. cut detail areas from folds before cutting out between the crystals.

Appliqué with Folded Cutwork: Anita Shackelford

Star

A star shape can be made from paper folded into fifths, sixths, or eighths. Fold the top layer of the paper one more time to create a center line. Begin the star point at this center mark and carry the lines to a point on each fold, the same distance from the center (2-42). Cut-out shapes can be added along the folds and may also be positioned on the center line.

Scherenschnitte designs can be ambitious projects when appliquéd. A traditional framed presentation for this style of work is shown in 2-43. Because the small motif was fused to the background instead of appliquéd, a more complex design could be used.

Rectangular Designs

Multiple-repeat designs can be cut to fill a rectangular space instead of a square. Folding is simplified for rectangular patterns because diagonal folds are not needed.

Two plus two

Begin with a rectangular piece of paper. Measurements should be based on the desired proportions and the finished size of the quilt. Fold the paper in half, and in half again in the opposite direction. From this double fold, patterns can be cut in a two plus two design style, in sizes for single blocks, for large medallion centers, or for wholecloth quilts with rectangular shapes. The cut for two plus two designs begins near the outside edge of one fold and ends near the outside edge of the other fold (2-44). The two parts of the design may be similar, or one motif may be much larger and more complex than the other. The interior of a cutwork medallion can be completely solid. It may have an open decorative center, or reverse appliqué areas can be added to create a filigree design (2-45).

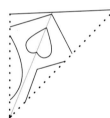

2-42. Cutting a single point on the open edge will produce an eight-pointed star scherenschnitte. Add details as desired along both folds.

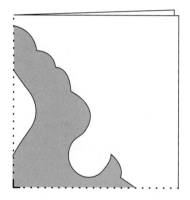

2-44. For two plus two designs, the paper is folded into quarters. Cut begins on one fold and ends on the other.

2-43. Scherenschnitte designs which are too small or intricate to appliqué can be fused to the background and framed in the traditional manner. 7" block.

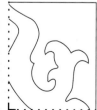

2-45. Detail can be added to interiors of two plus two designs with open centers, or other areas of reverse appliqué.

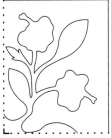

2-46. Tahitian Hibiscus, 40" x 60", designed and appliqued by the author, 1997. The one-quarter fold is used for most Tahitian designs.

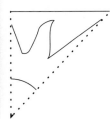

2-47. Use a compass to draw a true arc for a circular center opening as shown in the sun design.

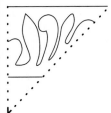

2-48. A single line drawn and cut perpendicular to the short fold creates a square opening.

Tifaifai

Traditional Tahitian designs, known as tifaifai, feature four asymmetrical repeats which often produce a rectangular design. To create a tifaifai, draw a large, complex motif within the one-fourth design space of the folded paper. The design may be connected at the folds or in the center and may have a minor motif on the short fold (2-46). Polynesian quilts generally reflect the flora and fauna of this tropical paradise, but you can personalize your tifaifai by creating a design that incorporates something familiar to your home and family.

Open Centers

Many of the previous patterns may benefit from having an opening cut in the center of the design. An open center can add detail, lighten a heavy design, or provide the perfect place for signatures in a friendship quilt. It is important that the center opening be separate from other cuts along the folds, so that it does not compromise the stability of the pattern.

Different shapes can be used to create a variety of center openings. Centers should complement the design style of the appliqué motif and should be the desired size for a signature or message that you may want to add.

Circle

To draw a circular center opening, put your pencil into a compass and set the measurement for the radius of the circle (half the desired size). For example, to mark a 4" circle, set the compass to measure 2". Draw the arc on the folded paper and cut along this line to cut a circular shape from the center of the paper template. Be sure that the center opening does not touch any of the cutout areas along either fold (2-47).

Square

A square opening will require one cut, perpendicular to the short fold. The length of the cut will be half of the desired size of the square opening. Position the end of a ruler on the short fold. Gradually move the ruler along the short fold until the measurement across the paper is half the size you want the opening to be. Draw a line along the top edge of the ruler and then cut on the line to produce a square opening in the center of the paper template (2-48).

Appliqué with Folded Cutwork: Anita Shackelford

A square on point can be made with a straight cut perpendicular to the long fold. To prepare this shape, position the end of a ruler on the long fold. Move the ruler along the fold until the measurement across the paper is half the size you want the opening to be. Draw a line along the top edge of the ruler and then cut on the line to create a square on point (2-49).

Octagon

To create an octagonal center opening, begin by measuring the same distance from the center to a point along each fold. This measurement should be half the size of the desired opening. Cut a line straight across the paper, between these two points, to produce an octagonal opening in the center of the paper template (2-50).

Stars

An eight-pointed star can be made by cutting a single star point into the center of the folded paper. First, fold the top layer of the paper to create a center line in the one-eighth space. Unfold the top layer and place a ruler along this line, measuring from the center of the paper to a point that is half the desired size of the center opening. Place a mark on the center line. Now measure the same distance from the center of the paper to the points along each fold; short measurements here will produce sharp star points, while longer measurements will create a larger opening. Draw lines that begin at these points on the folds and end at the common point on the center line (2-51). Cut along these lines to produce a star-shaped opening in the center of the paper template.

A six-pointed star can be made by measuring and marking in the same way if the paper is folded into six layers instead of eight (2-52).

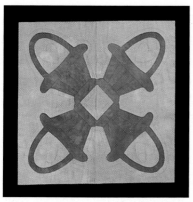
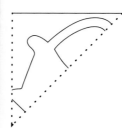

2-49. For square opening set on point, cut a single line perpendicular to the long fold.

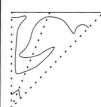

2-51. A star point cut into the center of the paper will produce an eight-pointed star.

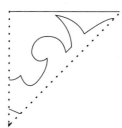

2-50. By drawing a single line across the center point of the folded paper, you can cut an octagonal opening.

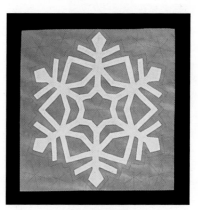

2-52. If the paper has been folded for a six-sided design, the same star point will produce a six-pointed central star.

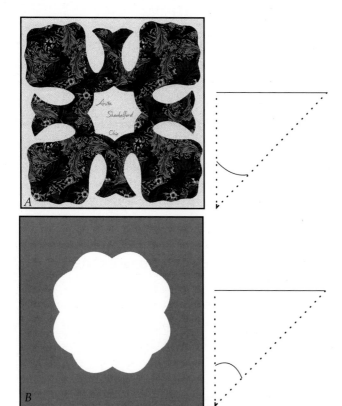

2-53. *A,B.* A curved line from one fold to the other will create a scalloped opening in the center of a design.

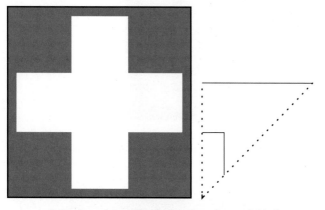

2-54. A rectangular shape, placed on a folded edge, will create an open cross in the center.

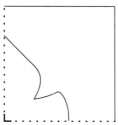

2-55. Medallions can be cut from the center of paper which has been folded into fourths.

Scallops

For a softly curved opening, begin by measuring the same distance from the center to a point along each fold. This measurement should be half the desired size of the center opening. Draw a line that gently curves in (2-53*A*) or out (2-53*B*). Cut along this line to produce a scallop-shaped opening in the center of the paper template.

Cross

An open cross can be cut into the center of a block by cutting a small rectangular shape from the center of the folded paper. The first line should be made perpendicular to the short fold. Make a square corner and continue the cut down to the long fold (2-54). For pleasing proportions, the second line should measure approximately twice as long as the first line.

Medallion

An open medallion with an arabesque shape can be made with a combination of corners and curves cut from the center of the paper. Medallions are probably more pleasing if they are cut as a two plus two design. Fold the paper in half, and in half again in the opposite direction, to cut this type of center opening (2-55).

Flower petals

A design with an eight-petal flower in the center can be made by cutting identical petal shapes from each fold. Use the simple symmetry technique (p. 15) to make a petal template and trace half of the petal on each fold, the same distance from the center (2-56*A*). A larger version of this design, with petals cut from the full paper, has been used as a signature block pattern in the past. Another variation on a flower shape includes an open circle in the center and rectangular petals cut from both folds (2-56*B*). Use the simple symmetry technique for the petals or cut them free-hand for a more natural look. Be sure that the center opening and the petals are isolated cuts that do not touch each other.

2-57. Traditional floral motifs grow from a cutwork center in a mid-nineteenth century appliqué quilt from Ohio. Courtesy of Xenia Cord, Kokomo, Indiana.

2-56A, B. A variety of flower centers and petals can create interesting openings in the centers of cutwork designs.

Combinations

A paper-folded pattern can be just the beginning of a more complex appliqué design. Cutwork designs can be combined to create a more complex image, appliquéd cutwork can be used in combination with other types of appliqué, or a cutwork motif can be the main element, which is then embellished with embroidery and other touches. Embellishing appliquéd cutwork also gives us the opportunity to use more than one color, which is important in floral designs. One traditional style of appliqué combines cutwork centers with floral motifs growing into the corners of the block (2-57). Blocks in this style are often seen in Baltimore album quilts and other mid-nineteenth century appliqué with Germanic roots.

A new design based on this idea combines a cutwork center with folk art flowers which grow to the corners and also to the sides of a large block. Not only is the center motif a cutwork design, but the flower, bud, and leaf templates for this pattern were also cut from folded paper (2-58).

2-58. A new block design includes cutwork center, flowers, leaves, and buds made with folded paper patterns.

Emily Senuta of Overland Park, Kansas, created an interesting design when she layered one cutwork shape on top of another. The first appliquéd layer is a four corners design with small areas of reverse appliqué to create a delicate look (2-59). The top motif is a four plus eight design with the four main elements positioned to lie in between the four motifs of the first layer (2-60). The four minor elements and the center design of the top layer overlap and interact beautifully with the layer below.

An antique red-and-green appliqué quilt, in the author's collection, contains a pattern with a center flower, large melon motifs, and buds (2-61). Although all of the pieces for this quilt were cut separately, they perhaps would have been more accurately aligned if the main motif had been cut as one piece. With this in mind, the individual shapes were traced from the original quilt and used to create a cutwork pattern in the four plus four

style. This new pattern was used to produce the red and green sample block shown in 2-62.

By studying the melon appliqué quilt, we can see how additional appliqué shapes might be used to add interest to any cutwork greenery. Ruth Kennedy and friends created an appliqué quilt that combines a cutwork pattern of stems and leaves with beautiful purple irises (2-63). The green and purple color combination is very pleasing and much more natural looking than a single color appliqué would have been.

Sheila Kennedy's friends added circular ruched flowers to a variety of folded cutwork designs to make FLOWERS FROM FRIENDS (2-64). Circular, heart-shaped, and lyre-shaped wreath designs are combined with traditional sprays of flowers that grow from cutwork centers. Ruched flowers add texture and dimension to the quilt.

2-59. Layered cutwork design used as the middle layer is a four corners cactus motif.

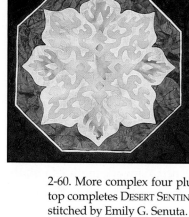

2-60. More complex four plus eight design on top completes DESERT SENTINELS. Designed and stitched by Emily G. Senuta.

2-61. Antique Melon quilt from author's collection.

2-62. Melon and Bud block redesigned as a four plus four cutwork. Center flower will be added separately.

Appliqué with Folded Cutwork: Anita Shackelford

The blocks of the FOUR SEASONS cover quilt demonstrate how appliquéd cutwork can be embellished in a variety of ways. The Spring block of iris is a four plus four design. Each flower is embellished with small ruched beards (2-65A). Summer is depicted by a circle of butterflies with simple embroidered antennae (2-65B). The Fall block was created with grape leaves in a four corners arrangement. Individual grapes were added, using a stuffed appliqué technique (2-65C). Winter holly is a four plus eight design which has been embellished with small free-form berries (2-65D). The embellishments add interest and realism to the appliqué in this quilt.

2-63. A more natural look is achieved when flowers and buds are separated from the cutwork motif and appliqued in a second color. THE IRIS GARDEN quilt is shown on p. 47.

2-64. Ruched flowers add color and texture to a variety of cutwork designs. FLOWERS FROM FRIENDS quilt is shown on p. 46.

A

B

C

D

2-65. *A.* Cutwork irises are embellished with small ruched beards; *B.* embroidered antennae add the finishing touch to appliquéd butterflies; *C.* a four corners grape leaf design is complemented by stuffed grapes; *D.* free-form berries accent a cutwork holly appliqué.

Appliqué with Folded Cutwork: Anita Shackelford

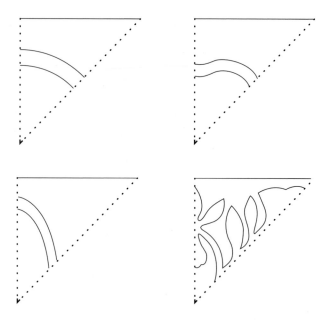

2-66. Base lines for wreaths can follow a variety of shapes.

2-67. Rose and Bud wreath follows a circular framework with repeating motifs placed on both the long and short folds.

Wreaths

Wreaths have long been favorite designs for all types of appliqué work. In most designs, branches, stems, leaves, and other motifs are cut separately and positioned on the block, one at a time. The folded cutwork technique can be used to create a wide variety of wreath designs that are cut all in one piece.

Appliquéd cutwork wreath designs can be simple or complex, but they have one thing in common. They are open in the center and attached at both folds. To begin a wreath, draw a curved line from one fold to the other. This line will determine the shape of your wreath. There are several shapes that a wreath might follow. The basic line may be round, scalloped, slightly curved, or it may follow a deep diagonal line across the paper (2-66).

Antique quilts sometimes contain a block with a wreath that looks more square than circular. If you want an accurate circle for the base or framework of a wreath, use a compass to scribe a true arc. To begin, set your compass for half the desired center opening size and mark the inside curve of the wreath. To this measurement, add the desired width of the wreath itself and use this setting to mark the outside curve of the wreath. Draw the design so that it follows the arc of these two lines. Motifs which are to repeat can be positioned on both folds (2-67).

A directional design cannot be cut from a folded paper pattern. A single motif positioned to follow the line of the wreath (2-68) will repeat itself in pairs. The ivy leaf design shown in 2-69 appears less directional because it has many small leaves pointing in several different directions.

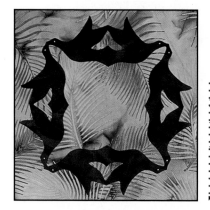

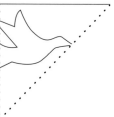

2-68. Doves in a circle demonstrate how a motif will be mirrored as it repeats around a wreath shape. Stitched by Emily Senuta.

2-69. Ivy wreath appears random and more natural.

Appliqué with Folded Cutwork: Anita Shackelford

A wreath can also be created by cutting a four corners design in which the motifs touch at the sides but do not extend into the center. In 2-70, an Hawaiian-style flower was placed on the long fold, near the open edge of the paper. Because the flower design extends across both folds, the flowers interlock to form a wreath.

Interlocked Designs

Non-botanical images, or other shapes which may not grow on a vine, can also be joined or over-lapped to form a wreath shape. The butterflies in 2-71 are placed in opposite positions on both the long and the short folds so that the tips of their wings over-lapped slightly. When this design is cut, it creates a ring of butterflies that appear to be in flight.

Frames

Another variation on the wreath shape is a frame that might be used for inked messages or placed around an appliqué picture or a photo transfer. Square frames should be attached on both folds and designed along lines that run perpendicular to the short fold. A guide line on the paper will ensure that the frame will fit. Measure the picture or message that is to be framed and decide on the inside measurement of the frame. Divide this measurement in half. Measure this distance from the center of the folded paper to a place along the short fold and make a mark. Draw a line from this mark, parallel to the outside edge, ending on the long fold. Centering the design lines of the frame on this guide line will produce a frame in the correct size (2-72).

The simplest frame might be a gentle swag that runs from corner to corner. The corner of the block is located on the long fold of the paper near the outer, open edge. Begin your design here. Place the swag or other design along the open edge of the paper, with the middle of the motif touching the short fold (2-73). When this design is cut and opened, you will have a square frame with four identical sides.

2-70. Island Beauty design, attached at sides and open in center, also has the appearance of a wreath.

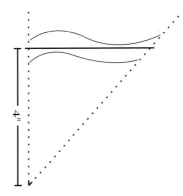

2-72. Measuring 4" from the center, along the short fold, will create a frame with an 8" opening.

2-71. Butterflies positioned on both folds overlap each other to form a wreath shape.

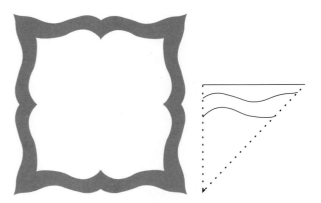

2-73. Frame follows guide line drawn perpendicular to short fold.

For a little variety, an additional motif, such as a heart, can be added to the corners. Use the same swag or a different shape for the long sides of the frame and place it along the open edge, as before. Add any simple shape centered on the long fold (2-74). When the piece is cut and opened, you will have a square frame with an identical motif in each corner.

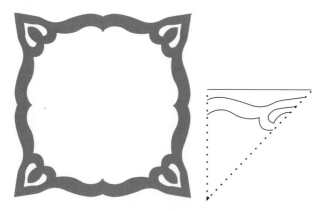

2-74. Motif placed on long fold will produce a frame with identical motifs in each corner.

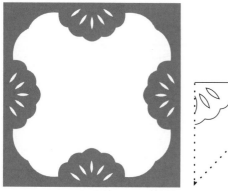

2-75. Motif placed on short fold will produce a frame with identical motifs at each side.

2-76. Complex design repeats in corners and along sides.

Frames can be designed with motifs centered along each side rather than in the corners. To create this type of design, position the long bars of the frame along the open edge, perpendicular to the short fold, as before. Adding a shell or flower motif on the short fold will create a frame with four identical motifs, each one centered along the sides of the frame (2-75).

You might consider cutting a design that combines one motif at the corners and others along the sides, such as that shown in Figure 2-76.

Frames can also be cut in rectangular or oval shapes (2-77). Begin with a rectangular piece of paper in the same proportions as the picture or finished center design. Fold the paper into fourths instead of eighths. As you position your chosen motifs, keep in mind that a motif that is placed on the long fold will be centered at the top and bottom of the frame; a motif that is placed on the short fold will be along each side (2-78).

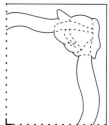

2-77. Rectangular frame with motif in corners, cut to fit around photo transfer. Scott and Jennifer Perdue. Made by the author, 1998.

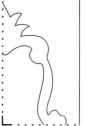

2-78. Rectangular frame with motifs positioned at top, bottom, and along sides. Author's grandfather, 1914.

Appliqué with Folded Cutwork: Anita Shackelford

Borders

Paper-folded patterns can be used in a variety of ways to design motifs which will fit the borders of a quilt. A small border can be folded and cut in the same way that frames are made. Because the border pattern is cut as one piece, it will have corners included and will fit perfectly (2-79).

Simple symmetry swags can be positioned at intervals along the length of a border. These motifs can be positioned with space between them, or they might be connected by swag spacers (2-80). Repeated motifs can also touch each other as they repeat around the border. The design might be cut so that motifs are connected to each other along the outer edge of the border (2-81) or within the design itself (2-82). Cutwork designs can also be planned so that combinations of different motifs can be repeated in pairs or even three at a time (2-83).

To find the size of a motif to repeat along the full length of a border, measure the border and find the numbers that divide easily into the total measurement. For example, 80" can be divided evenly by 10", 8", 5", 4", and 2". Therefore, motifs that fill any of those divisions will repeat evenly along a border measuring 80".

2-79. Center medallion bordered with a ribbon pattern.

2-81. Tree border is connected at edge of quilt.

2-80. Border swags can be designed with or without space between them.

2-82. Teddy bears touch paws as they repeat along the border.

2-83. Two different motifs can be designed to alternate with each other.

Border design styles

Simple symmetry

For a single motif that repeats its way along a border, use the simple symmetry technique to create a template such as a swag or leafy sprig. Use paper measured to the length and depth the motif is to fill. These individual motifs may touch each other, or they may be separate as they make their way around the quilt. The chosen design will be centered across a single fold and cut to produce a motif with symmetrical halves (2-84).

Pairs

The simple symmetry technique can also be used to create a pair of motifs that will be a pleasing repeat in a border. Taking inspiration from nineteenth-century woven coverlets, a pair of kissing birds repeated at intervals could be added to a country or folk art style quilt. Pairs of motifs are planned on paper with a single fold. Instead of centering the design across the fold, position the motif so that it just touches at the fold. In LITTLE BOY DREAMS, a full bird motif was cut from each layer of the paper, producing a pair of birds that are connected to each other (2-85).

Symmetry with a center motif

A design with a center motif plus a full repeat on each side can provide a larger and more interesting border repeat. The dog and tree pattern is similar in style to the design of the pillow sham shown on page 18. A single fold is used to cut a symmetrical design with a center motif. Position the design so that the center motif is on the fold and the repeating asymmetrical motif is cut from the remainder of the paper (2-86).

The repeating pattern of flowers and leaves shown in 2-87 was cut in this same style. The flower is a simple symmetry motif that was cut on the fold. The pair of leaves were cut from the full body of the paper and repeat on each side.

2-84. Leafy swag was designed with the Simple Symmetry technique. Detail from FLOWERS FROM FRIENDS quilt shown on p. 46.

2-85. Motifs in pairs can be created by positioning a full motif so that it touches the fold.

2-86. Symmetrical designs with a center motif can be repeated at desired intervals along a border.

2-87. A. The flower and leaves pattern is an example of a design with a center motif; B. this design can also be connected with a stem or vine for a full running border.

Paper folding for full border repeats

Moving into a paper-doll style of cutwork, paper can be folded to create a template that is connected and repeated for the full length of the border. To ensure the fit of a complex border design, it may be safer to cut a paper template for the full pattern. Begin with the measurement for the full border and find a reasonable size for the desired repeat. For example, the length of the teddy bear border in 2-88 is 20" and the size of the motif is 4" so that it will repeat five times.

Make a master pattern in the size of a single repeat. Fold the full length of paper into as many layers as necessary to produce the number of repeats needed. Folding the paper accordion-style (2-89) may produce more accurate units than repeatedly folding it over on itself. On long borders, you may find that there are too many layers of paper to cut easily. Use the master pattern to mark and cut the design through just a few layers of paper at a time. When the entire border pattern has been cut, check the fit and placement along the edge of the quilt. Complex borders should be designed and cut with this method.

Single motif

Long borders can be filled with a series of connected cutwork motifs repeated at intervals to fill the space, as shown in the detail photo of an antique quilt, which has a single tree design repeated along an entire border (2-90). To find the size of the repeat in a border such as this, figure the measurement of one motif plus the distance to the next one (2-91). Make your master pattern from paper this size. Fold the paper in half to cut a single symmetry motif. The repeating motif will be positioned across the fold and connected along the open edge. Fold the border paper into the necessary number of repeats and trace the design from the master pattern onto the border paper. Cutting the design from a folded paper template will ensure even spacing of the motifs.

2-88. Four-inch teddy bears repeat evenly to fill length of border. Full border shown on p. 82.

2-90. Single tree motif is repeated at regular intervals along full border of an antique quilt.

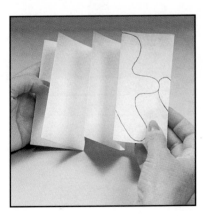

2-89. Fold border paper accordion-style for more accurate border repeats.

2-91. For a motif which is connected at the edge of the quilt, position the repeating motif on the fold and carry the connecting ground line to the opposite side of the paper.

Alternating repeat

Cutting a different motif from each fold will create a design in which the motifs alternate with each other along the length of the border. Make a master pattern from paper in the size of the desired repeat. Draw two motifs with each one centered on a fold. The two motifs can be the same size (2-92*A*) or different sizes (2-92*B*) depending on the amount of paper used for each one. Fold the paper into the necessary number of repeats and trace the design from the master pattern. When the design is cut through all layers, the two motifs will be symmetrical shapes that will alternate along the length of the border.

A

B

2-92. Details from LITTLE BOY DREAMS (quilt shown on p. 82); *A*. same size motifs in an alternating repeat; *B*. alternating different size motifs.

Triple repeat

It is possible to make three different motifs repeat along a border by cutting one on each fold and the third from the center of the paper. Because the center motif is not cut on a fold, it allows us the opportunity to use an asymmetrical shape in that space (2-93). Begin with paper for a master pattern in the size of the desired repeat. Position a different motif to be cut from each fold and a third motif between them. Use the master pattern to transfer the design to folded units of the border paper.

Running designs

As discussed in designs for wreaths, a directional, flowing design cannot be cut from a multiple-fold pattern. If a directional or asymmetrical design is cut on a fold, it will mirror itself as it repeats along the border. One solution to developing a running border is to use an angled placement for a single motif. These motifs will repeat in pairs but can be cut as a continuous design, as shown in the border of a cutwork quilt made by Susan Nicholson (2-94). If the motif itself is symmetrical end to end, it can be connected and will not appear to change orientation as it repeats.

An undulating ribbon design will also flow along a border and around the corners without appearing to be directional. A small ribbon pattern was cut in one piece for a perfect fit around the center eagle medallion in LITTLE BOY DREAMS (pg. 82).

2-93. Three different motifs can be made to alternate along a border by placing one motif on each fold and the third motif between them.

Appliqué with Folded Cutwork: Anita Shackelford

HAPPY ANNIVERSARY, BILL

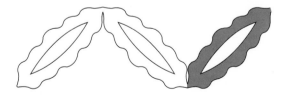

2-94. HAPPY ANNIVERSARY, BILL, 82"x 82", made by Susan Denton Nicholson, Muskegon, Michigan, 1996. Four plus eight center connects to a four corners design to fill each block of this large four-block quilt. Angled placement of leaves was used to create a running border design.

2-95. Leaves positioned to repeat across a lengthwise fold create a directional running border design, used here as a quilting pattern in FOUR SEASONS (quilt shown on p. 68).

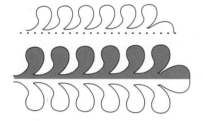

2-96. Feathers in any size or style can also be repeated across a lengthwise fold.

2-97. Detail from 1860s REVISITED (quilt shown on p. 48). Swag spacers connect border motifs and eliminate the need for perfect measurements.

Lengthwise fold

A different style of directional design can be cut from paper with a single fold that runs along the length of the border. A simple leaf design cut on a lengthwise fold (2-95) will be mirrored side to side within the border. As with the simple symmetry style, the motif may be repeated as many times as necessary to fill the space. Feathers might be cut and repeated side to side, in this same way (2-96).

Swag spacers

Swag spacers are simple, symmetrical motifs that can be used in combination with swags or with other border design elements. If you plan a border that includes these little in-between motifs, you will find that perfect measurements are not necessary and adjustments are easy. The spacers will help to guarantee even placement along the length of a border by filling the extra space between the primary design elements. The flower and calyx design works well as a swag spacer in the border of a quilt made by Jo Lischynski and friends (2-97). Other motifs, such as a simple bow, a triple bow, finials, and tassels, can be used in this way (2-98).

2-98. Bows, tassels, and other small motifs make pleasing swag spacers.

Appliqué with Folded Cutwork: Anita Shackelford

Corners

When designing continuous borders, corners can be left open or filled with a separate motif. Borders can also be butted together, or the design can be planned to flow around a mitered corner. Trees form a continuous border on each of the three sides of an antique cutwork quilt. The borders were butted together for square corners, and the appliqué design follows the same format (2-99). The leafy swags on Sheila Kennedy's border were planned as separate motifs with space between each one.

The swags were repeated to fill the length of the border, and the corners were filled with an additional flower motif (2-100). Two other ways in which a design can be planned to fit a mitered corner are shown in 2-101. The pine tree motif (2-101A) has a shape that fits perfectly into each corner, while the gingerbread men and hearts (2-101B) turn the corner as a continuous design. If a quilt is planned with different designs in each border, the corners may not be continuous but may be left open as in the top corners of LITTLE BOY DREAMS (2-102).

2-99. Antique mid-nineteenth century red and green folded cutwork appliqué quilt with continuous cutwork border. Trees on quilt follow butted corner design.

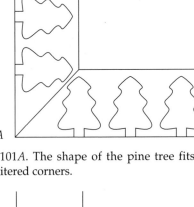

2-101A. The shape of the pine tree fits into mitered corners.

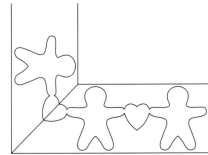

2-101B. The heart motif turns the corner between the gingerbread men.

2-100. Detail from FLOWERS FROM FRIENDS. A small flower motif was used to fill the corner between leafy swags.

2-102. Detail from LITTLE BOY DREAMS. Corners can be left open if designs are different from border to border.

FLOWERS FROM FRIENDS

FLOWERS FROM FRIENDS, 72" x 72". This beautiful album quilt includes a variety of blocks which combine cutwork greenery and ruched flowers. The border includes leafy swags along the sides and small single flowers which fill the corners. Designed by the author, hand appliquéd by Sheila Kennedy and friends, Glenda Clark, Janet Hamilton, Ruth Kennedy, Jo Lischynski, Connie St. Clair, Rebecca Whetstone, and the author. Hand quilted by Barbara Yoder, Wayne County, Ohio. Collection of Sheila Kennedy, Bucyrus, Ohio, 1998.

Appliqué with Folded Cutwork: Anita Shackelford

THE IRIS GARDEN

THE IRIS GARDEN, 80" x 80". Combination cutwork adds natural color and a sense of realism to a beautiful iris appliqué. Designed by the author, hand appliquéd by Ruth Kennedy and friends, Glenda Clark, Judy Gammell, Janet Hamilton, Sheila Kennedy, Jo Lischynski, Velora Mowry, Connie St. Clair, and Rebecca Whetstone. Hand quilted by Sarah Yoder, Wayne County, Ohio. Collection of Ruth Kennedy, Fremont, Ohio, 1998.

1860s Revisited

1860s Revisited, 80" x 96". Four plus eight blocks alternate with combination cutwork in this vibrant quilt. The blocks are set in a Garden Maze design and finished with a swag border which includes spacers. Designed by the author, hand appliquéd by Jo Lischynski and friends, Glenda Clark, Janet Hamilton, Ruth Kennedy, Sheila Kennedy, Joan Longbrake, Connie St. Clair, Rebecca Whetstone, and the author. Hand quilted by Barbara Yoder, Wayne County, Ohio. Collection of Jo Lischynski, Green Springs, Ohio, 1998.

Appliqué with Folded Cutwork: Anita Shackelford

3 GETTING STARTED

part three

GETTING STARTED

COLOR AND DESIGN

There are many things to consider when choosing fabrics for appliqué. Color produces the most immediate response; choose colors that you like and that work well together. The fabrics chosen for the appliqué and the background should have good value contrast so that the cutwork image is clear and strong. Fabrics can be chosen to set a mood. Consider whether you want a controlled palette, a scrap look, or a period piece. The following quilts and samples will give you an idea of the exciting possibilities that await when you are ready to translate your folded cutwork designs into appliqué.

3-1. CUTWORK APPLIQUÉ, 81" x 81", by the author, 1990. A single color appliqué simplifies the task of creating a balanced arrangement. Hand appliquéd and hand quilted.

Appliqué with Folded Cutwork: Anita Shackelford

Color

A limited selection of fabrics or colors may work best when used with a large variety of appliqué designs. Using only a single appliqué fabric throughout a quilt makes it very easy to arrange (3-1). With uniform color, the only planning that is required is a balanced layout of the blocks.

For a little more variety, consider using a collection of designer prints which have the same scale and value. The dark prints used in FOUR SEASONS are similar to each other in value and scale and all contain a gold accent (3-2). Different prints were chosen to reflect the mood of each season. Because the fabrics will appear very similar at a distance, the blocks will be as easy to arrange as those made from a single fabric.

The variety available within a group of reproduction prints from a single designer series can add visual interest to a sampler quilt without looking too busy or confusing. Although the prints in FRIENDSHIP ALBUM vary somewhat in color and value, their common style adds unity to the quilt (3-3).

If the designer series you love does not have a great variety of prints, consider using a limited number of fabrics and repeating them throughout the quilt. If you decide on only a few favorite prints that work well together, use each of them several times to make the required number of blocks.

3-2. Details from FOUR SEASONS. Fabrics of similar value and scale add visual unity to this quilt (full quilt shown on p. 68).

3-3. FRIENDSHIP ALBUM, 1998. A large selection of fabrics from William Morris designer series has a variety of color and scale, while a similar style adds unity. Blocks appliquéd by Virginia Anderson, Bonnie K. Browning, Patricia B. Campbell, Darlene C. Christopherson, Cindy Cimo, Glenda Clark, Patricia Ulbrich Flath, Lois French, Janet Hamilton, Irma Gail Hatcher, Ellen Heck, Jane Holihan, Ruth J. Kennedy, Sheila Kennedy, Jo Lischynski, Marjorie Lydecker, Phyllis D. Miller, Susan Denton Nicholson, Victoria Paradise, Doreen Perkins, Marie Salazar, Connie St. Clair, Emily Senuta, Anita M. Smith, Judy Spence, Beverly Jane Stellges, Sharon Stroud, Katharine Stubbs Ward, Rebecca J. Whetstone, and the author.

Many colors can be made to work well together if they are combined into a planned and balanced arrangement, such as RAINBOW, made by Helen Karl (3-4). Colors move across the quilt in a pleasing manner and the use of only solid colors helps to unify the quilt.

A scrap look which uses a great number of fabrics is perhaps most effective with a single appliqué pattern, as shown in the OAK AND ACORN quilt. Colors which set a fall mood also help unify this quilt. The prints used include some leaf designs and tie-dye fabrics, while others contain geometric, painterly, or formal designs. The colors chosen for the quilt are primarily green, gold, orange, and brown but also include small amounts of the complementary colors red, violet, and blue. While some combinations are close in value, a contrasting thread color helps to define the edge of the appliqué. Because the value contrast occasionally changes between foreground and background, the overall quilt has a subtle positive/negative effect.

The combination of large leaf and small acorn creates a motif which does not fill the sides of the block completely. Positioning this image side by side has produced a secondary pattern with a pleasing curvilinear effect (3-6).

Value

Value is defined as the lightness or darkness of a color. Fabrics chosen for appliqué should have good value contrast with the background. A sample oak and acorn block shows little contrast in fabrics, with similar color and value in the foreground and the background (3-5A). Stronger value contrast helps define the shape of the appliqué in 3-5B.

3-4. RAINBOW, 86"x103", made by Helen Karl, collection of Theodore S. Karl. A large sampler of Hawaiian style designs shows a very effective arrangement of the full spectrum of colors.

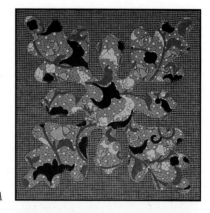

A

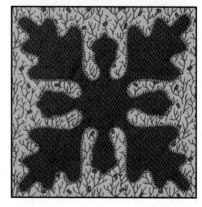

B

3-5. Value. *A*. Poor contrast between appliqué and background; *B*. good value contrast defines the design.

Appliqué with Folded Cutwork: Anita Shackelford

OAK AND ACORN

3-6. OAK AND ACORN, 81" x 90", by the author, 1997. A true scrap quilt, every appliqué and every background fabric is different. The use of only one motif allows the focus to be on the fabric choices. Machine blanket stitch appliquéd, hand and machine quilted.

Scale

Scale refers to the size of a print on a fabric. Be cautious of large-scale prints, with dramatic color and value change when choosing appliqué fabrics. If the background of the appliqué fabric or a color within the print is similar to the color of the background block, those areas may seem to disappear at the edges of a motif, and the shape of the appliqué may be lost (3-7A). Large scale prints which have good value contrast with the background will be a better choice (3-7B).

Directional Prints

If the print of the appliqué fabric is directional, think about how you can use it for its best effect. One sample block shows an appliqué motif cut from a single piece of fabric with the directional print running vertically (3-8A). Another sample was made with the directional print radiating from the center of the motif (3-8B). To make a template for this type of radiating design, copy ¼ of the pattern and add seam allowance to the edges where the pieces will be joined (3-8C). Position the template on identical parts of the printed fabric to cut each section of the motif. Cut out the shapes with the seam allowance as marked; add seam allowances to the appliqué edges. Join the sections to produce a cutwork design with a kaleidoscope effect.

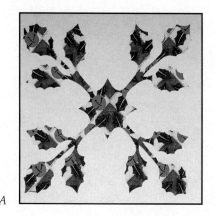 

A   B

3-7. *A.* Shape of holly leaves is lost by using large-scale print with coloring similar to the background; *B.* large-scale print will work if colors have good contrast with background.

  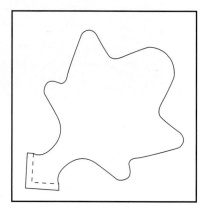

A   B   C

3-8. *A.* Directional print placed vertically in cutwork design; *B.* directional print used in a radiating pattern; *C.* seam allowance added to make template for piecing a radiating design.

Mood

Fabrics can be chosen to create a certain feeling or mood. Although Hawaiian and Tahitian quilts are traditionally made with solid colors for both appliqué and background, think about choosing fabrics that will set a tropical mood. Bright colors and foliage designs can lend a Polynesian feeling as shown in the four-block wall quilt in 3-9.

Sometimes the fabric itself will determine what type of design should be cut from it. Ethnic prints might be used to create a quilt which will remind you of a special place. An Australian fabric printed in the pointillist style of Aboriginal painting was a good choice for an appliquéd cutwork of kangaroos (3-10). Look for seasonal prints to cut designs for holidays or special occasions (3-11). Cutwork patterns can also be designed to coordinate with the theme of certain juvenile or novelty prints such as the frogs on the lilypads in 3-12.

Study the fabric selections used in the sample quilts throughout the book. Whether you like mid-century red and green, turn-of-the-century darks, 1930s pastels, or tropical brights, choose fabrics which will set a mood and make your quilt in the style that you prefer.

3-10. Australian fabrics fit the theme for an Aboriginal-style kangaroo.

3-11. Christmas fabrics help set the mood for ANGELS AND TRUMPETS, designed by Ann Connors, and made by the author, 1998.

3-9. Careful selection of fabrics enhances the mood of these designs. Blocks stitched by Linda Gabrielse, Velora Mowry, Katharine Stubbs Ward, and the author.

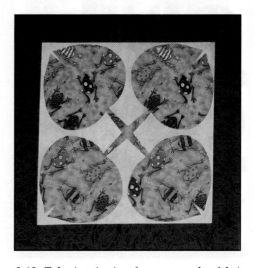

3-12. Take inspiration from a novelty fabric and develop a coordinating appliqué design.

Folding and Cutting Accurate Templates

When you are ready to cut your final paper template for appliqué, follow these important steps to ensure that the folds are even and the shapes are cut as accurately as possible.

1. Fold the paper carefully. Match the edges exactly and press each fold firmly with your thumbnail or the side of a pencil to make a sharp crease.

2. If you are tracing the design, place a small mark on the top layer of the folded paper to indicate the section of the paper where the design should be traced. Open the paper and place the marked section on top of the pattern. Match the fold lines of the paper to the edges of the pattern.

3. Trace the design carefully and refold the paper so that the drawn pattern is visible on the outside layer.

4. If you are drawing your own design, remember that any pattern, no matter how small or complex, will need a minimum of ¼" space between motifs to allow for an ⅛" seam allowance to be added along each side when the piece is cut from fabric (3-16A,B).

5. Use bridges in the paper pattern to connect small motifs which eventually will be isolated as the fabric piece is cut and appliquéd (3-17).

6. Staple several places close to the design, in the background only, to prevent the layers of paper from slipping during the cutting process (3-18).

7. Use small sharp scissors or an X-acto knife and cutting mat to cut out the design. Be sure to hold the scissors or knife blade perpendicular to the paper, not slanting in or out, so that all of the layers will be cut uniformly. When cutting with scissors, hold the scissors in place and guide the paper into the blades. Use the full length of the blades to make long cuts, rather than a short choppy motion which may produce uneven edges.

8. Hold the scissors under the paper when cutting toward your dominant side and above the paper when cutting away from your dominant side. For example, if you are right-handed and cutting a line which curves toward the right, the scissor handles should be beneath the paper; when cutting a line which curves toward the left, the scissor handles should be above the paper (3-19A,B). This position allows the cutting edges of the blades to make the best contact with the line being cut.

9. Cutting into sharp corners from both directions, whenever possible, will be more accurate than pivoting the scissors around an inside point.

10. On an outside corner, it is all right to cut past the corner, as long as the cut extends into the background. This extension will allow a more accurate placement of the scissors to begin the next cut.

11. Use a paper punch to make an opening for the scissors in areas of reverse appliqué (3-20).

12. For stability in complex designs, cut detail areas first before cutting away outside edges which have been stapled.

13. If major design elements appear too heavy, re-fold the paper and cut a slightly narrower shape until a pleasing pattern is obtained. As an alternative, cut an opening within the motif to create a lighter feeling (3-21).

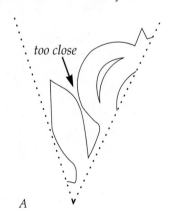

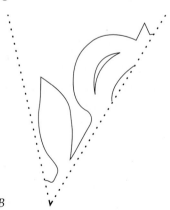

A   B

3-16. Pomegranate. *A.* Design lines placed too close together; not enough room to cut seam allowance; *B.* design re-drawn with adequate space between motifs.

Bridges
are shaded

3-17. Bridges hold the sections of a pattern together until they are appliquéd. The bridges are cut away individually as the appliqué is done.

3-18. Staples keep paper from shifting as it is cut.

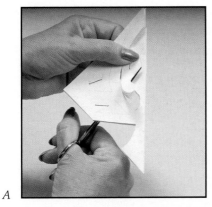 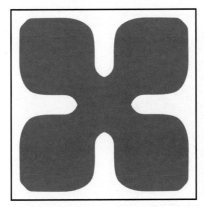 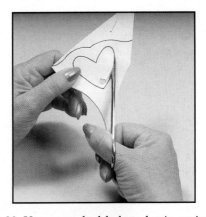

A

B

3-19. *A.* Hold handle of scissors underneath paper when cutting toward dominant side; *B.* hold handle of scissors above paper when cutting away from dominant side.

3-20. Use a punched hole to begin an isolated cut.

3-21. Re-cutting, or adding open areas, can lighten a heavy design.

CUTTING THE APPLIQUÉ MOTIFS

Folded Fabric Technique

The Polynesian technique for preparing shapes for appliqué includes folding the fabric into fourths or eighths and cutting through all the layers of fabric at one time to produce the repeated, symmetrical image. TAHITIAN HIBISCUS (p. 30) was cut this way. There are several advantages to the folded fabric technique. Obviously, a complete pattern for such a large motif will require a large piece of paper, while a pattern for one-fourth or one-eighth of the design will be smaller and more manageable.

Working with only a small part of the pattern requires confidence that the full design will be pleasing and the ability to cut an accurate shape through so many layers of fabric at one time. Be sure to use a pair of scissors that will cut evenly through all of the layers. The time and work involved in cutting the appliqué from folded fabric are only one-quarter or one-eighth of what would be required to cut a full shape from a single layer of fabric.

If the appliqué piece is to be cut with only the paper as a guide, there will be no need to find a marker which will show on the fabric and no time spent in tracing the outline. Without a marked line to follow, the seam allowance will be turned by eye as the appliqué is stitched. Some quiltmakers may feel this is a disadvantage, but with large, complex, asymmetrical designs, small differences won't show. Practice and experience will lead to confidence in turning a uniform, narrow seam allowance.

Before cutting a design in this way, prepare the appliqué fabric by starching it lightly as it is pressed. The starch will give the fabric more body and make it easier to control. Fold the fabric, right sides together, into as many sections as the pattern requires, pressing the layers together after each fold (3-22A). If you are folding into eighths, remember that the butterfly fold will be more accurate than folding the diagonal folds

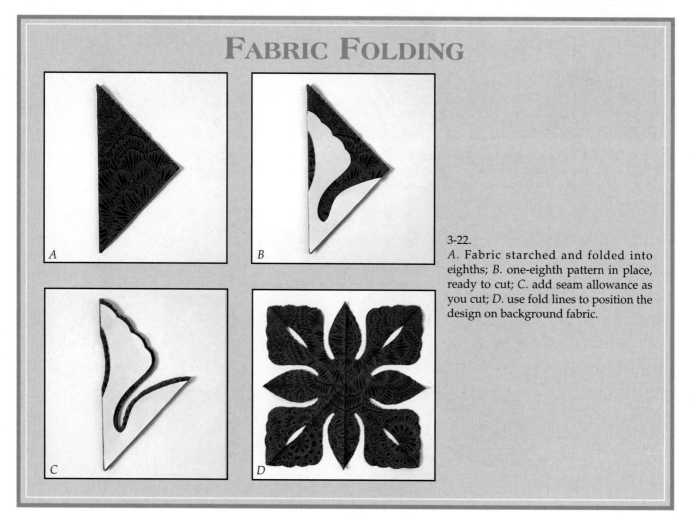

FABRIC FOLDING

A

B

C

D

3-22.
A. Fabric starched and folded into eighths; *B.* one-eighth pattern in place, ready to cut; *C.* add seam allowance as you cut; *D.* use fold lines to position the design on background fabric.

all in one direction. Fold and press the background fabric in the same way to create guide lines for positioning the appliqué piece. When choosing a design to be cut in this way, consider that there is some advantage to a tifaifai design, which is cut four layers at one time, rather than a design which requires the fabric to be folded into eighths.

Pin the paper pattern to the folded appliqué fabric, matching the center and the folded edges carefully (3-22*B*). Place pins in the background areas also, to keep the layers of fabric from slipping as they are cut. Use small sharp scissors to cut out the appliqué design, adding a narrow turn-under allowance all around (3-22*C*).

Unfold the background fabric and secure it to a flat surface, right side up. Handle the cut appliqué piece carefully to avoid stretching bias edges. Because the appliqué fabric has been folded right sides together, it can be positioned on the background and unfolded one layer at a time (3-22*D*), matching the fold lines to those on the background fabric.

If the design is very large, open, or complex, it may require extra care in keeping the elements properly aligned until it is basted to the background block. The piece can be positioned by eye and then, if needed, measured to check the distance from the fold lines and between the individual elements.

A large appliqué piece can be secured to the background in a variety of ways. Pinning the piece into place is not very effective as the pins may fall out during the handling of a large piece and there is also the risk of being stuck by the pins as the stitching is done. Basting the layers together will hold the appliqué securely and will make it easier to handle. Place the line of basting at least ¼" in from the raw edge to allow a minimum ⅛" seam allowance and ⅛" margin under which to turn it (3-23). A water soluble glue can also be used to set layers together and prevent them from shifting as the appliqué is done.

Freezer Paper Patterns

A full pattern, cut from folded paper, is a good choice for making the smaller designs for block-style appliqué. Any paper will work (3-24) but a plastic-coated freezer paper pattern ironed onto the fabric can provide more accuracy in marking and cutting out an appliqué shape because it will not move as the design is being traced. There are several approaches to preparing patterns, transferring the design to the fabric, and appliquéing the pieces into place. As you read through the options, you will see that choices may be made based on the complexity of the design and your preferred appliqué technique.

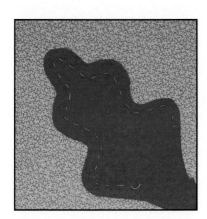

3-23. Motif basted in place on background block.

3-24. Early twentieth century paper-fold pattern cut from newspaper. Collection of Jo Lischynski, Green Springs, Ohio.

Marking around the template

Marking around a template is the most common way to transfer a design onto the appliqué fabric. Unfold the freezer paper pattern and iron it onto the right side of the fabric (3-25A). Draw around the pattern to create an accurate outline. Remove the paper and cut out the appliqué shape with a narrow seam allowance added (3-25B). Edges may be pre-basted at this point, if you prefer (3-25C), or the piece may be appliquéd with the needle-turn technique. Position the appliqué piece on the background, matching the quarter and eighth fold lines. This technique will work well for simple shapes, but complex designs may be floppy after they are cut and can be difficult to position accurately.

For more control of a complex shape, leave the freezer paper in place while the appliqué is being cut and positioned on the background block (3-25D). To begin, iron the freezer paper onto the right side of the appliqué fabric. Draw around the pattern but do not remove the paper. Cut out the appliqué, adding a narrow seam allowance all around. Position the cut-out motif on the background block. Leaving the paper on the fabric adds body to the piece, making it easier to handle and position correctly. Leaving the pattern in place can also be a very helpful visual guide when trimming away the background on a complicated filigree motif. Remove the paper a little at a time and pin the motif to the background, being careful to match the quarter and eighth fold lines. Use the needle-turn technique to appliqué the motif in place.

MARKING AROUND THE TEMPLATE

3-25.
A. Freezer paper template, ironed into place, will not shift as it is traced; B. cut out appliqué motif, adding a narrow seam allowance all around; C. edges pre-basted in preparation for appliqué; D. leaving the freezer paper on while the motif is cut adds stability when positioning the appliqué piece on the background.

Appliqué with Folded Cutwork: Anita Shackelford

Cut-away appliqué

For more accurate placement of a complex design, the appliqué shape may be cut a little at a time, as it is being stitched. As before, iron the freezer paper onto the right side of the appliqué fabric. Draw around the pattern for an accurate turn line. Remove the paper, but do not cut out the design. Position the marked appliqué block on the background block (3-26). Using small sequin pins, pin the two layers of fabric together within the appliqué shape. Adding a narrow seam allowance, cut out the appliqué shape a little at a time and use the needle-turn technique to stitch it into place.

Freezer paper attached during appliqué

Leaving the freezer paper on the fabric as the stitching is done can add stability and shape to the appliqué piece. The freezer paper may be ironed onto either the right side or the wrong side of the appliqué. If you plan to appliqué with the paper on top, iron the freezer paper onto the right side of the appliqué fabric. Position the uncut appliqué fabric on the background block. Secure the blocks together with pins placed in the background areas. Trim and needle-turn the seam allowance a little at a time, using the edge of the paper as a guide (3-27). Remove the paper template when the appliqué is complete. There is no need to mark an outline with this technique. The paper template can be removed and used again.

If you prefer to appliqué with the paper underneath, iron the freezer paper onto the wrong side of the fabric. Cut around the paper template, adding a narrow seam allowance. Position the appliqué shape on the background block and pin to hold it in place. Needle-turn the seam allowance around the edge of the freezer paper and stitch the motif in place. Turn the block to the wrong side and cut away the background block behind the appliqué to remove the freezer paper (3-28). If the pattern is removed carefully, it may be used again.

Starch-and-press

The starch-and-press technique can also be used for preparing appliqué edges. For this process, begin by pressing the freezer paper pattern to the wrong side of the appliqué fabric. Cut out the motif with a narrow seam allowance added all around, clipping into all of the inside corners and curves, as needed. Brush a line of liquid starch along the seam allowance. Use a hot iron to turn the seam allowance around the paper template and set it into place. When the edges are dry, remove the paper pattern and pin the appliqué motif into place on the background block. The block is ready to stitch and the paper template may be used again if desired.

3-26. Cut-away appliqué technique; background of appliqué fabric is cut away and seam allowance is turned a little at a time.

3-27. Freezer paper template can be left in place while the appliqué is stitched.

3-28. If appliqué is done with the freezer paper underneath, the background must be cut and the paper pulled out.

TIMES AND SEASONS

TIMES AND SEASONS, 61"x76", by the author, 1997. A calendar quilt with cutwork appliqué blocks designed to represent special holidays and the change of seasons. Twenty-four hand dyed fabrics were used for the blocks and repeated in the inner border. Machine blind stitch appliquéd, hand and machine quilted.

Appliqué with Folded Cutwork: Anita Shackelford

SHIP'S WHEEL

SHIP'S WHEEL, 73½"x80". Unusual four corners and two plus two designs are appliquéd onto a whole cloth background in an early twentieth century quilt from Maine. Author's collection.

SNOWFLAKE

SNOWFLAKE, 78" x 78". Collection of Marilyn Woodin/Woodin Wheel Antiques, Kalona, Iowa. Sampler quilt shows a great variety of folded cutwork styles. India ink inscription on back of quilt: "This quilt was made by Mabel Likes and Anne Morris and bought (the square patches) by Mrs. G. G. Knowles and made by her and quilted for her daughter Mrs. Henry Grant to whom this quilt is presented by her Mother, October 10th, 1868."

Appliqué with Folded Cutwork: Anita Shackelford

4

THE TECHNIQUES
part four

THE TECHNIQUES

APPLIQUÉ TECHNIQUES

There are many different appliqué techniques from which to choose, depending on the type of quilt you are making, its intended use, or the amount of time you have available. Included here are complete step-by-step photos and instructions on the needle-turn technique and blind stitch appliqué by hand (4-1). Hand appliqué can also be done with a running stitch or blanket stitch. By machine, you can blind stitch or use the cut-away appliqué method with decorative stitches. Fused appliqué edges can be finished by hand or machine. Add to your appliqué skills by trying a sample of each.

4-1. FOUR SEASONS, 28½" x 28½", by the author, 1998. Each block uses a different style of cutwork design, combined with dimensional appliqué or embroidery embellishment for added interest and realism. The border quilting patterns were also designed with folded cutwork techniques. Hand appliquéd and hand quilted.

Blind Stitch by Hand

Most of my cutwork is appliquéd using the needle-turn technique and a blind stitch. Done properly, this stitch should live up to its name and not be visible. Begin by choosing a thread that matches the color of the appliqué fabric or a color and value that will not show on the finished piece. It is difficult to hide a thread that does not match, no matter how good your stitches are. Sometimes you may not be able to find an exact thread match. If you must choose between a slightly lighter or slightly darker thread, choose the darker. Usually a darker thread recedes; a lighter thread is more apt to advance and be more visible. Choose a fine needle to do any type of hand appliqué. As a general rule: the smaller the needle, the smaller the stitch. A large needle will not easily penetrate several layers of fabric and may bump the seam allowance out of place, causing the edge to be uneven.

Make a knot in the end of the thread and trim the tail, if necessary, to prevent it from shadowing through. As the needle comes up from behind the block, it should catch just the very edge of the appliqué piece (4-2A). To make the next stitch, take the needle down through the background only, right beside the stitch which just came up. Advance along the underneath surface, with the needle parallel to the edge, and come up again, piercing the edge of the appliqué piece as before (4-2B). The thread should not advance on the top, but simply wrap over the edge of the patch. If pulled with the proper tension, the thread should drop down into the weave of the appliqué fabric and be hidden. Appliqué stitches should be small, tight, and close together (4-2C) to hold the piece firmly in place, but not so tight as to cause distortion.

BLIND STITCH

4-2.
A. Needle comes up through edge of appliqué; B. blind stitch is taken with needle parallel to edge of appliqué; C. back of block shows stitches are small and close together.

Needle-turn Technique

Large flat pieces with corners and fine points are often easiest to appliqué by using the tip of the needle to turn under the seam allowance, so this technique of needle-turn appliqué is perfect for appliquéd cutwork. With the needle-turn technique, the appliqué piece is secured to the background block and the seam allowance is turned under as the stitching progresses around the edge (4-3A, p. 70). A Sharp or Milliner needle will provide good control for the combination of needle-turn and blind stitch appliqué. Try several types of needles to see which one feels right in your hand.

For needle-turn appliqué, the motif should be cut with a seam allowance which is ⅛" to ³⁄₁₆" wide. Pin or baste the motif into place on the background block. The seam allowance will be turned under as the stitching progresses around the piece. Do not try to turn the edge of the motif very far ahead of the place where you are stitching. You will have best control of the edge if you turn only enough for two or three stitches at a time.

The needle-turn technique sometimes creates the problem of surface distortion if the appliqué piece is allowed to move as the seam allowance is turned. Basting or pinning close to the edge where you are working (4-3B) will help avoid pushing the fabric out of place. Little sequin pins can be placed close to the edge without interfering with the work.

Inserting the point of the needle into the seam allowance will give you better control for the needle-turn technique rather than using the needle to sweep the edge under. Control is the key word here. Catching hold of the seam allowance with the point of the needle (4-3C) will allow you to turn the edge under as far as needed or to ease it out again if it has been turned too far. Repeatedly sweeping or pushing the edge under can cause it to ravel or to be uneven. Stick the point of the needle into the seam allowance; it should never need to touch the raw edge.

NEEDLE-TURN

4-3. *A.* Use tip of needle to turn seam allowance under; *B.* small sequin pins hold appliqué in place; *C.* insert point of needle into seam allowance for better control when turning edge under.

Outside square corner

Turning an accurate outside corner is simple if the corner is square or nearly so. Needle-turn the first edge and appliqué it all the way to the marked corner. Do not try to turn the second edge until the first side is completely secured. Catch the needle into the seam allowance of the second edge and pivot it around the last stitch to tuck it into place (4-4). Because the second fold can sometimes turn under too far, tug lightly on the thread to pull the corner out to a good point before taking the next stitch. Continue your appliqué along the second side.

4-4. Stitch first side to corner; use needle to pivot next edge around and under.

Appliqué with Folded Cutwork: Anita Shackelford

Sharp point

There are several reasons that appliqué points are not sharp and neat. Too much fabric is a common problem; a wide seam allowance will simply not fit underneath a fine point. If the point is not folded properly, the tip may be square or rounded in shape. Too much bulk placed beneath the tip can make it rounded or lumpy.

The seam allowance must be turned with three separate folds to make a sharp point. To begin, needle-turn the first edge and stitch it all the way to the marked point. As with the outside square corner, do not try to turn the point until the first side is completely secured. Some very sharp points will have a small tip of fabric which extends beyond the seam allowance on the unsewn side. Lift the edge of the appliqué and trim away this little tip, even with the other raw edge (4-5A). The second fold turns the tip under; the folded edge should be straight across, perpendicular to the point (4-5B). Take a stitch at the very tip to hold this second fold in place (4-5C).

The third fold will turn the remaining edge under. It would seem simple enough to pivot this edge around the stitch and under in the same manner as the square corner, but this sometimes creates too much bulk under the tip. A slightly different approach can create a smoother finish. Rotate the piece, so that the tip of the appliqué is pointing directly at you. Hold the needle so that it also points toward you. With the point of the needle, catch hold of the seam allowance at the tip and use the needle to slide the raw edge under and, at the same time, away from the tip (4-5D). Use your thumb on top to hold the layers together and, without letting go of the piece, put in at least one stitch to hold the seam allowance in place (4-5E). With the tip completely secured, you can turn the piece around to a more comfortable stitching position and continue.

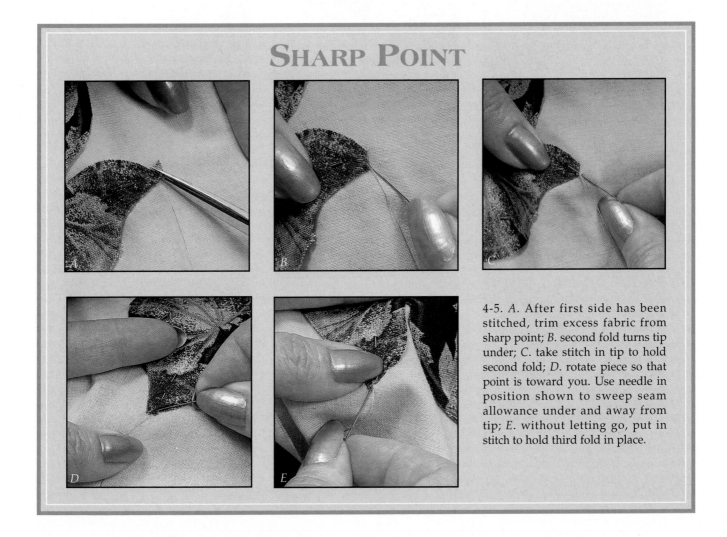

SHARP POINT

4-5. *A.* After first side has been stitched, trim excess fabric from sharp point; *B.* second fold turns tip under; *C.* take stitch in tip to hold second fold; *D.* rotate piece so that point is toward you. Use needle in position shown to sweep seam allowance under and away from tip; *E.* without letting go, put in stitch to hold third fold in place.

Inside Corners

Inside corners and V shapes need just one clip straight in, to within a thread or two of the turn line (4-6A). Both square corners and deep V shapes can be turned and stitched in the same manner. Stitch along the first side to within one or two stitches of the corner. Use the needle to turn under the seam allowance of the other edge and pin it or hold it in place with your thumb.

Use the needle again to sweep around the inside corner and roll the seam allowance under (4-6B).

One problem in stitching an inside corner is that the needle can no longer run parallel to the folded edge. As the stitch is taken across the corner, the needle hits the far edge head-on and can cause the edge to lift and the seam allowance to come out. Instead of stitching across the corner in the conventional manner, use a stab stitch (4-6C) for the next two or three stitches. The single up and down stitches are less traumatic and seem to encourage the seam allowance to roll under as the stitch is taken. These stitches are not deeper and should not show. However, they may be placed closer together for better control of the edge.

Inside Curves

Inside curves need to be clipped for ease in turning the seam allowance just as inside corners. For a narrow curve, clip a little crow's foot at the end (4-7A). The extra side clips will allow the opening to soften for a more rounded shape. Gentle concave or inner curves will also require a little give in the seam allowance in order to turn under smoothly. A series of small cuts, perpendicular and almost to the marked line, will allow the seam allowance

INSIDE CORNERS

4-6. A. Make one clip straight into inside corner; B. use needle to roll seam allowance under at inside corner; C. a stab stitch at inside corner will encourage seam allowance to roll under.

INSIDE CURVES

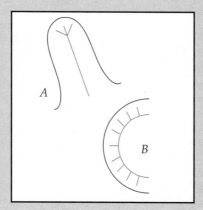
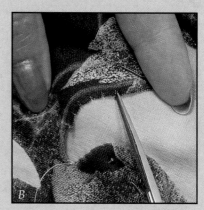

4-7. A. Clipping a crow's foot will add ease to a narrow inside curve; B. make a series of clips along a gentle concave curve.

Appliqué with Folded Cutwork: Anita Shackelford

to fan out when it is turned under (4-7B). A bias edge on an inside curve will also make the seam allowance easier to turn and easier to control because it will not ravel.

Outside Curves

It is not necessary to clip outside curves. With careful turning, the seam allowance can be eased under between stitches. On very small pieces or tight curves, you may need to adjust the position of the seam allowance after every stitch. Catch the needle into only a single layer of the seam allowance and gently pivot it around the last stitch (4-8). Do not fold over both layers as you did in turning a corner or you will create a little point along the edge.

Reverse Appliqué

If a motif has detail areas, as in the filigree cutwork or open centers, these small areas should be worked after the outside edge of the appliqué is stitched into place. Use a sharp, little scissor point to lift the appliqué piece away from the background block to cut out these areas. Add a seam allowance, inside the drawn line, as you cut away each shape (4-9A). These areas of reverse appliqué will allow the background block to show through, or for variety, another fabric can be placed behind the open area for a color accent (4-9B).

The reverse appliqué technique can also be used to set an entire cutwork motif into the background block. Prepare the freezer paper pattern in the same way as for appliqué on top (see p. 63). Iron the pattern onto the right side of the background block and mark around it. Remove the paper and layer the marked background block on top of the fabric which will show through. Carefully cut out the inside shape where the paper pattern had been, adding a seam allowance inside the drawn line. Clip all inside points and curves and use the needle-turn technique to appliqué the background into place around the design (4-10). Choose a thread color which will match the fabric on top, which in this case, is the background fabric.

Reverse appliqué may offer several advantages and also presents its own unique problems. Cindy Cimo, an appliqué instructor from Medfield, Massachusetts, loves

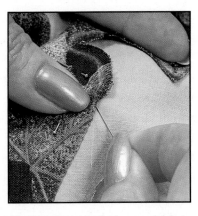

4-8. Catch only a single layer of fabric and ease it back under the previous stitch to turn a smooth outside curve.

4-9. A. Seam allowance must be added inside drawn line for reverse appliqué areas; B. additional color added behind reverse appliqué areas in Sunflower block.

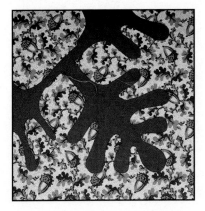

4-10. Reverse appliqué technique used to set a full motif into the background block.

reverse appliqué (4-11) and feels that the technique gives her work a smoother finish. Turning seam allowances toward the outside of the block, rather than toward the center as would be done with appliqué on top, may produce a flatter appliqué piece.

Some quiltmakers find it easier to needle-turn and sweep the inside curves and points instead of turning points on the outside edges. Study the pattern to see if there are more inside or outside points and which ones are sharper. Surprisingly, in some designs, there is a difference. Make this decision based on your own skills.

If the background fabric is a solid color or a subtle print, it will be easier to draw an outline that will show on this fabric rather than on a busy print. Only one thread will be needed to match the background instead of many colors which would be required if the motifs are of varying colors. Placing very dark fabrics behind light background blocks generally causes a problem with shadow through, which can be distracting in the finished piece. A darker value for the background fabric will help conceal this shadowing. If you must layer light fabric over dark, trim carefully, to remove as much excess fabric as possible.

When tying off stitches in the background fabric behind the appliqué, be sure that you know which side of the stitching line is the double layer, as it is different for reverse appliqué. Be certain that these stitches do not come through to the right side of the block.

4-11. FLEUR DE LIS MEDALLION, 34" x 34", by Cindy Cimo, Medfield, Massachusetts, 1997. Made with the reverse appliqué technique.

Blind Stitch by Machine

Consider using the freezer-paper-underneath method to prepare motifs which will be appliquéd with an invisible machine stitch. The freezer paper pattern provides an accurate shape and also adds stability for machine stitching.

Begin by ironing the freezer paper pattern to the wrong side of the fabric. Cut out the motif, with a seam allowance added all around. Clip into all the inside curves and points as for hand appliqué. Wrap the seam allowance around to the dull side of the paper and use a water soluble glue stick to hold the seam allowance in place (4-12A). Position the prepared appliqué on the background block and secure it with pins. Use a close, narrow zigzag and nylon thread to machine appliqué the motif into place. When the stitching is finished, cut away the background fabric behind the appliqué motif. Soak the block in warm water to loosen the glue and remove the paper. Machine appliqué with freezer paper underneath produces an accurate design with a smooth, flat finish (4-12B). The TIMES AND SEASONS calendar quilt (p. 64) was appliquéd with this technique. Even when you consider the time spent preparing seam allowances, this is much quicker than hand appliqué. With this technique, the paper pattern will be pulled out in pieces and will not be reusable.

Fused Appliqué

Most instructions for fused appliqué suggest that the motif be drawn onto the paper side of the fusible sheet. Because the fusible web cannot be folded for tracing and cutting a pattern, a method must be used to transfer a full design to the fabric or to the paper backing. A freezer paper template which can be folded and cut all at once will work as well to prepare a piece for the fused appliqué technique as it does for blind stitch appliqué. Begin by pressing the fusible web to the wrong side of the appliqué fabric. Press the freezer paper pattern to the right side of the fabric and cut out the design by cutting around the paper template, with no additional seam allowance. Remove the freezer paper pattern from the top and the paper backing from the fusible web and position the appliqué motif on the background block. Follow the manufacturer's directions for the fusible web you are using to fuse the appliqué into place. With this technique, the freezer paper pattern can be reused a few times.

Appliqué with Folded Cutwork: Anita Shackelford

Another idea is to cut a full paper pattern and trace it onto permanent template material. Trace around the template to transfer the design to the paper side of the fusible web (4-13A). There is no need to reverse the template as the design is symmetrical. Press the fusible web to the wrong side of the appliqué fabric. Cut out the motif on the marked lines. Remove the paper backing and fuse the appliqué into place on the background block (4-13B). This method works well for images that will be repeated many times. After the appliqué has been fused into place on the background block, work a blanket stitch or other decorative stitch over the raw edges, by hand (4-13C) or by machine (4-13D).

BLIND STITCH BY MACHINE

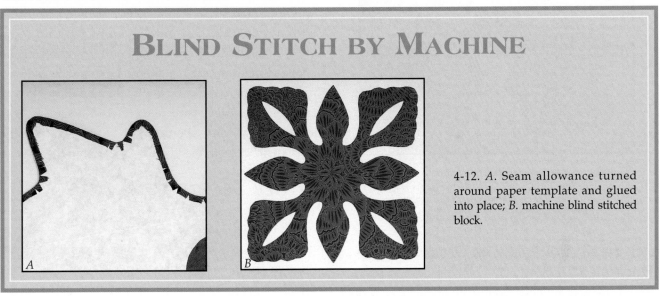

4-12. *A.* Seam allowance turned around paper template and glued into place; *B.* machine blind stitched block.

FUSED APPLIQUÉ

4-13. *A.* Motif traced onto paper side of fusible web; *B.* appliqué fused into place; *C.* hand blanket stitch worked in crewel wool; *D.* machine blanket stitch over edge of fused appliqué.

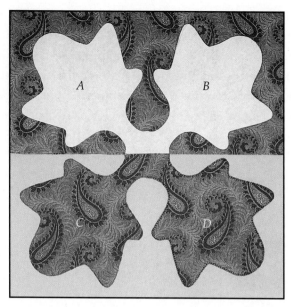

4-14. *A.* Iron freezer paper pattern onto fabric; *B.* machine baste outline motif to background; *C.* cut away background fabric; *D.* finish edge with decorative stitching.

Cut-away Appliqué with Decorative Machine Stitching

Cut-away appliqué requires no marking, no fusible web, and no seam allowance to be turned. For this approach, prepare a folded freezer paper pattern and iron it onto the right side of the appliqué fabric (4-14*A*). Place the appliqué block on top of the background block and pin the blocks together in the background areas. Use a straight stitch and matching thread to baste a careful outline of the appliqué motif, following the edges of the paper pattern (4-14*B*). You will be stitching the two layers of fabric together, but do not stitch through the paper pattern. When the stitching is finished, remove the pattern and cut away the excess appliqué fabric close to the basting line (4-14*C*). Use a machine satin stitch or other decorative stitch over the basted edge to appliqué the motif into place (4-14*D*). With the cut-away machine appliqué technique, the pattern may be saved and used again.

Visible Running Stitch

Banners made from wool or acrylic felt can be appliquéd without turning under the edges. This easy appliqué method is a good technique for beginning quilters. Some of the samples in 4-15 were made by children without much previous stitching experience. Quiltmakers with arthritis or carpal tunnel syndrome may also find it easier to work with a larger embroi-

dery needle rather than the fine needle used for traditional blind stitch appliqué. Felt appliqué is a good choice for complex shapes with many sharp points, such as the Christmas cactus block, since there is no worry about turning under a seam allowance.

To prepare a piece for running stitch appliqué, press the freezer paper pattern onto the right side of the appliqué piece. Use a moderate heat when working with acrylic felt. Cut out the motif with no seam allowance added. Remove the pattern, and pin the appliqué motif in place on the background block. Use a running stitch and a double ply of embroidery floss to appliqué the piece into place (4-16). Because these stitches show, they should be the same size and the same distance from the raw edge all around the piece.

OTHER TECHNIQUES

Stencil Painting

When folded paper is cut for an appliqué motif, the remaining background paper contains the same design, as a negative image. This left-over paper can be used to mask a background block for painting the design onto fabric (4-17*A*).

Prepare and mark a folded, freezer-paper pattern in the same way as for traditional appliqué. If you need to staple layers together, do not staple into the background since this is the piece that will actually be used. Use extreme care when cutting the design to cut smooth edges and keep the background paper intact. Do not allow the cuts to extend beyond the design into the background area. When the design has been cut, set aside the central motif; this template can be used for traditional appliqué. Unfold the remaining paper and fuse it firmly to the background block. It is important to have a firm seal at the edges to resist the paint and give the design a clean shape. When painting, be careful that the brush does not lift the edge of the paper. Brush from the paper onto the fabric, rather than from the fabric to the paper, to help keep the edges of the paper pattern secure. Allow the paint to dry, remove the paper, and heat set the paint according to the paint manufacturer's directions. Stenciled cutwork can be designed to stand alone, or it may be further embellished with embroidery or other appliqué techniques (4-17*B*).

Appliqué with Folded Cutwork: Anita Shackelford

A

B

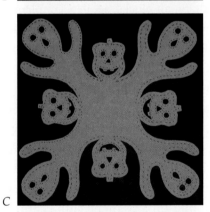

C

D

4-15. Holiday banners made with Kunin acrylic felt and running stitch appliqué. Blocks were stitched by A. Renée Whetstone, age 13; B. Rachel Whetstone, age 18; C. Nancy Miller, age 8; D. the author.

4-16. Detail of running stitch with double ply of embroidery floss.

A

B

4-17. A. Background of cut paper design used as resist in stencil painting; B. stenciled tree embellished with ruched roses.

4-18. A QUILTER'S BLESSING, designed by the author and screen printed by Elisa Shackelford, 1997.

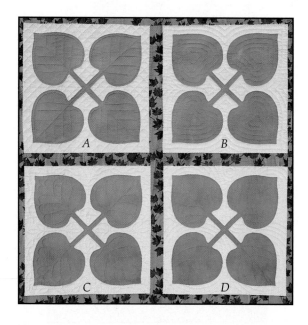

4-19. *A.* Traditional line and grid quilting creates nineteenth century look; *B.* echo quilting inside the appliqué and in the background is traditional Hawaiian pattern; *C.* feather and vine motifs create a more romantic style; *D.* botanical details such as leaf veins add sense of realism.

Silk Screen Printing

Adapting the stencil idea, my daughter Elisa used a cutwork pattern to make a silk screen and then screen printed the image onto a T-shirt (4-18). Silk screen printing is the technique to use for designs that you wish to repeat many times.

QUILTING

Tahitian appliqué quilts are left unquilted since the warmth of layers is not needed in a tropical climate. You might consider doing the same and finishing your top as a summer spread without a batting layer.

Background Quilting

Traditionally, Hawaiian appliqués are quilted in a wave or echo pattern with ½" spacing between the lines. The same pattern is used in the background and within the appliqué motif itself.

Appliquéd cutwork done in other styles might have background quilting that relates to that particular style of quilt. Small blocks, set in a sampler style, might have a single outline or double echo, with the background filled with any variety of line or grid pattern. Consider diagonal lines, double or triple lines, a grid, or a broken plaid in the background areas.

A wall quilt with the same appliqué motif quilted four different ways (4-19) demonstrates how the choice of quilting can change the look of the piece and perhaps set a mood. In the first sample, a four corners redbud leaf was quilted with a traditional line and grid which might be found on any nineteenth century appliqué quilt (4-19A). The second block shows traditional Hawaiian-style echo quilting within the appliqué and in the background areas (4-19B). A romantic or fantasy look was achieved with the use of feather and vine motifs to fill the leaves and the background of the third block (4-19C). The fourth sample was quilted with natural vein lines in the leaves for a sense of realism (4-19D).

The antique melon quilt shown in 4-20 was finished with echo quilting in lines ½" apart. The lines are placed within the motif as well as in the background, adding texture to the piece.

My large coxcomb was quilted in a nineteenth century manner with a double echo around each motif and a broken-plaid grid in the background (4-21). A large feather design fills the sashes between the blocks.

Appliqué with Folded Cutwork: Anita Shackelford

Quilting the Motif

The appliqués in the CUTWORK SAMPLER (4-22) were quilted with details that accentuate each motif. The quilting was finished with lines ¼" apart, echoing each motif and completely filling the background space.

It was surprising to find the unusual flower and vine pattern in the background of the SHIP'S WHEEL quilt from Maine (4-23). The quilting is very fine, with ten to eleven stitches per inch. The appliqué motifs have no quilting but are outlined with a ¼" echo line. The meandering background pattern appears to be somewhat random but was designed to fit the space.

The TIMES AND SEASONS calendar quilt includes detail within each appliqué which relates to the design of the appliqué motif (4-24). The background was finished with minimal quilting of a single outline in the ditch plus a ¼" echo line.

4-22. Background of CUTWORK APPLIQUÉ quilt is completely filled with ¼" echo quilting (quilt is shown on p. 50).

4-23. Unusual flower and vine quilting was used to fill background areas of SHIP'S WHEEL (quilt is shown on p. 65).

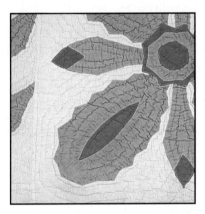

4-20. ½" echo quilting in an antique Melon quilt.

4-21. Coxcomb quilted with ¼" echo around appliqués and broken plaid in background.

4-24. Spiderweb quilting fits the theme in Ghosts and Pumpkins block (quilt is shown on p. 64).

Appliqué with Folded Cutwork: Anita Shackelford

Jo Lischynski designed beautiful quilting details to add to the appliqué motifs in her 1860s REVISITED (4-25). Quilting in contrasting thread also adds to the impact of this design.

Ruth Karl added a soft triple echo with ½" spacing around each of the Hawaiian style appliqué motifs in her beautiful RAINBOW quilt (4-26). The lines fill the background and add unity to this sampler quilt.

Rather than choosing separate designs for quilting the appliqué and the background areas of her four-block eagle quilt, Susan Nicholson created a very pleasing visual effect with overall fan quilting (4-27).

4-25. Fine detail quilting shows beautifully when stitched in contrasting color (quilt is shown on p. 48).

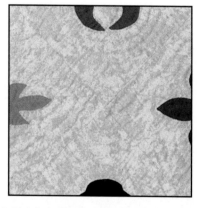

4-26. Triple echo line quilted around each appliqué (quilt is shown on p. 52).

Cutwork Designs as Quilting Patterns

Think about cutting original designs to fill an alternate block, side triangle, border, or other open space in a pieced or appliquéd quilt. Cutting your own patterns will guarantee that they will be the right size to fit the space.

A thistle pattern which was originally cut for an appliqué motif was instead used as a quilting pattern in the side triangles of the CUTWORK APPLIQUÉ quilt (4-28). If you have patterns which seem too complex to appliqué or which do not work as well with the others because of visual weight or balance, consider using them for quilting patterns.

A full ribbon border was cut to fit around the small PRECIOUS PETALS wall quilt. Cut from one piece of paper, the template was a perfect fit (4-29). The freezer paper was ironed onto the quilt and used as a guide for machine quilting the border pattern in this small quilt.

The four plus eight holly design from the FOUR SEASONS quilt (p. 68) was enlarged slightly and used to fill an alternate block in a pieced Christmas table runner (4-30). Padded and stuffed trapunto techniques have been used to add slight dimension to the quilted motifs.

A cutwork motif may be just the beginning of a more complex quilting design as shown in the grapevine border in 4-31. A single grape leaf made with the simple symmetry technique was the inspiration to design this border quilting pattern.

Whatever your interest in appliqué, there is certain to be a style of folded cutwork that will fit your plans. Folk art, Hawaiian-style, and many other appliqué quilts can be created by using cut paper designs. Cutwork motifs can be used to create a full quilt or can be combined with other appliqué blocks to personalize an album quilt. Even an all-white, whole-cloth quilt could be designed in this way. Once you start cutting folded designs you will be hooked. Pick up the scissors, relax, and enjoy the freedom of creating your own designs.

4-27. Fan quilting lends an antique feeling.

4-28. Thistle pattern with fine detail as quilting design in side triangle blocks.

4-29. PRECIOUS PETALS, 17" x 17", made by the author, 1998. Full frame freezer paper border, cut as one piece, fits perfectly. Hand and machine quilted.

4-30. Four plus eight holly motif used as a quilting design in Christmas table runner.

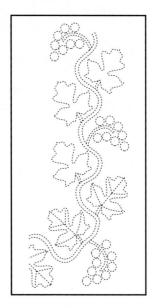

4-31. Simple symmetry grape leaf used to design border quilting pattern.

MIDNIGHT BLUE

MIDNIGHT BLUE, cutwork appliqué motifs create an eye-catching edge treatment on a garment made by Connie St. Clair, Helena, Ohio, 1998. Hand appliquéd, hand beaded, and machine quilted.

LITTLE BOY DREAMS

LITTLE BOY DREAMS, 46"x46". A medallion quilt made for my grandson, Brandon, utilizes a number of border styles. Motifs include simple toys, an eagle for strength and courage, and symbols of nature and the great outdoors – things that a little boy's dreams are made of. Hand appliquéd, hand quilted. Made by the author, 1998.

Appliqué with Folded Cutwork: Anita Shackelford

5 THE PATTERNS
part five

THE PATTERNS

More than 100 patterns are provided for your use as designs for appliqué, stencil painting, silk screen printing, quilting, or other uses you may choose. Only one section of each design is given. You will need to fold paper, according to the format of the design, to prepare a complete pattern. The designs can be used just as they are or you can add other elements to them.

Once you've selected a pattern, spend a few minutes reviewing the instructions in the Study of Design Styles section. Experiment with paper before you start working with your fabric. Every cut will teach you something new. Practice, in this case, leads you to new and exciting designs. Feel free to make adaptations in these designs or use them as a starting point for creating your own unique patterns.

TIPS FOR PAPERCUTTING PATTERNS

- Fold paper in sections (½, ¼, ⅕, ⅙, or ⅛) as described on the pattern.
- Dotted lines on the patterns represent folded lines.
- Dashed lines on the patterns represent suggestions for quilting .
- Dashed and dotted lines represent a break in the pattern, sections will need to be matched for a complete pattern.
- Match the center, the long fold, and the short fold of your paper with the pattern; the folds should lie exactly over the dotted lines on the pattern.

The patterns in this book may be copied for your own personal (non-commercial) use, including making a quilt and entering it in a quilt show where ribbons or monetary prizes are awarded. Credit should be given to the author anytime a quilt or its likeness using these patterns is shown.

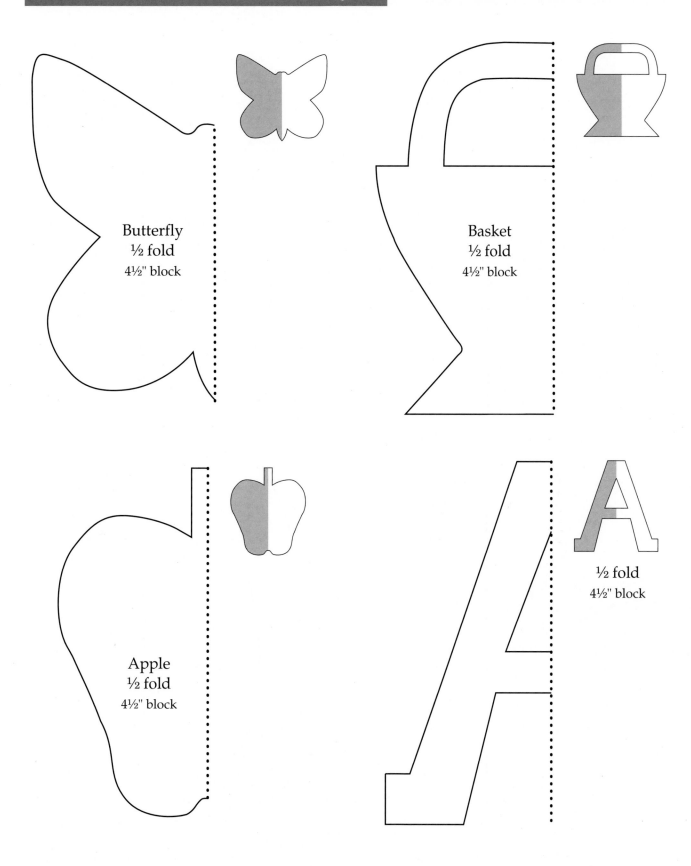

Butterfly
½ fold
4½" block

Basket
½ fold
4½" block

Apple
½ fold
4½" block

½ fold
4½" block

· · · · Fold Line • - - - Quilting Line • —— Cutting Line • -·-· Joining Line

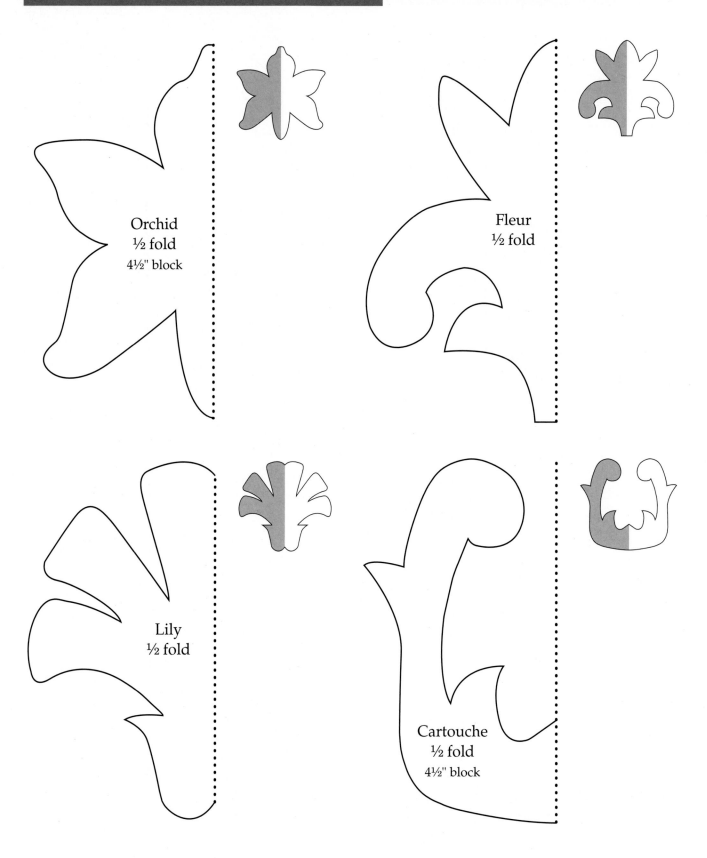

Orchid
½ fold
4½" block

Fleur
½ fold

Lily
½ fold

Cartouche
½ fold
4½" block

· · · · Fold Line   •   - - - Quilting Line   •   —— Cutting Line   •   -··— Joining Line

Appliqué with Folded Cutwork: Anita Shackelford

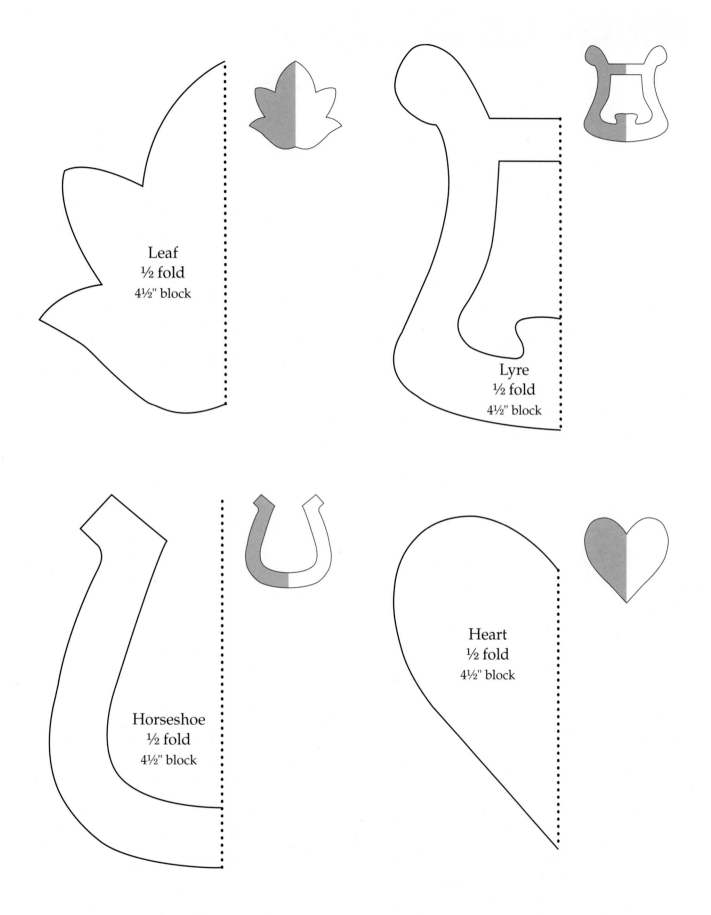

Leaf
½ fold
4½" block

Lyre
½ fold
4½" block

Horseshoe
½ fold
4½" block

Heart
½ fold
4½" block

· · · · Fold Line   •   - - - Quilting Line   •   —— Cutting Line   •   -··- Joining Line

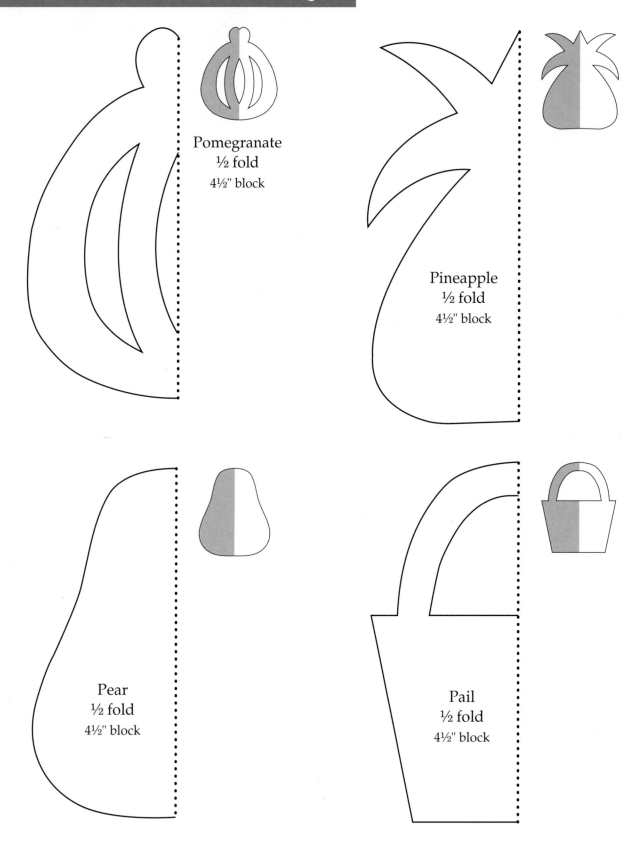

Pomegranate
½ fold
4½" block

Pineapple
½ fold
4½" block

Pear
½ fold
4½" block

Pail
½ fold
4½" block

· · · · Fold Line   •   - - - Quilting Line   •   ——— Cutting Line   •   -·-· Joining Line

Appliqué with Folded Cutwork: Anita Shackelford

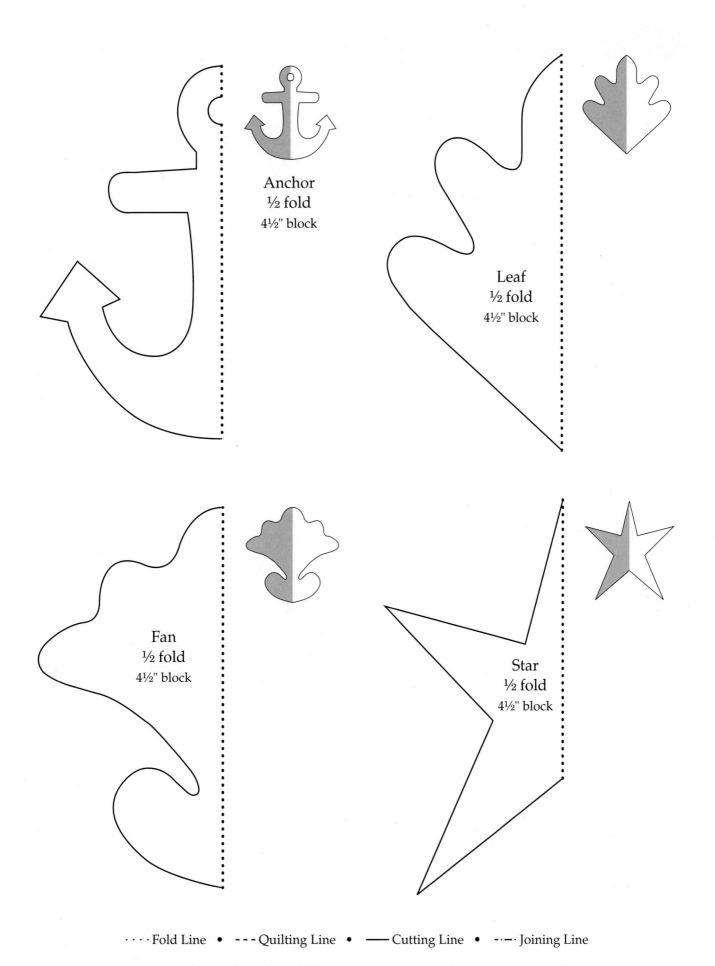

Anchor
½ fold
4½" block

Leaf
½ fold
4½" block

Fan
½ fold
4½" block

Star
½ fold
4½" block

· · · · Fold Line • - - - Quilting Line • —— Cutting Line • -··- Joining Line

½ fold
16" x 18" block

A join to B

· · · · Fold Line • - - - Quilting Line • —— Cutting Line • –·– Joining Line

B join to A

½ fold
16" x 18" block

Shaded areas are bridges to hold motifs
in place until you are ready to
appliqué that section.

· · · · Fold Line • - - - Quilting Line • —— Cutting Line • -·-· Joining Line

top

A join to B

½ fold • 14" x 18" block

· · · · Fold Line   •   - - - Quilting Line   •   —— Cutting Line   •   -·-· Joining Line

Appliqué with Folded Cutwork: Anita Shackelford

B join to A

½ fold • 14" x 18" block

· · · · Fold Line   •   - - - Quilting Line   •   —— Cutting Line   •   - · - Joining Line

Appliqué with Folded Cutwork: Anita Shackelford

93

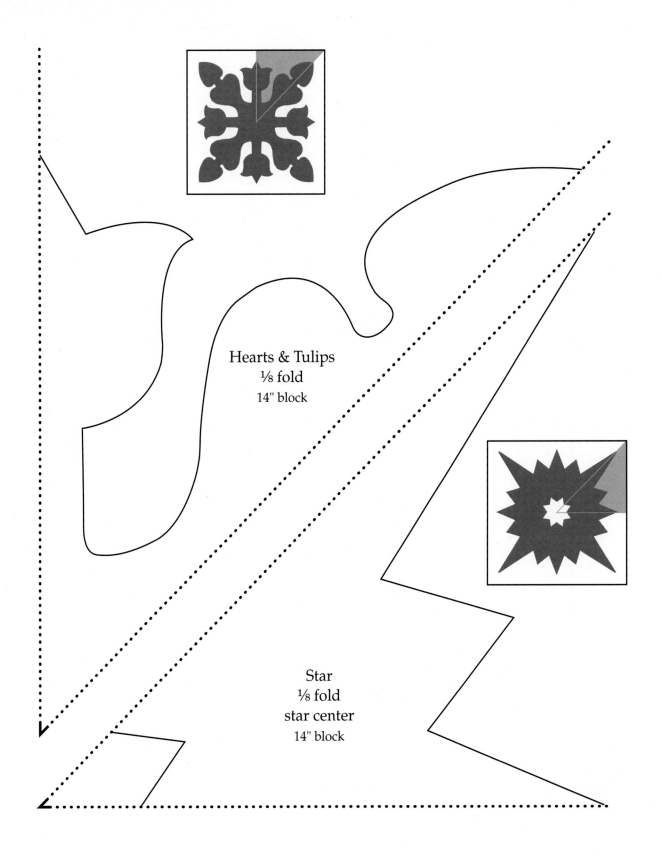

Hearts & Tulips
⅛ fold
14" block

Star
⅛ fold
star center
14" block

· · · · Fold Line   •   - - - Quilting Line   •   —— Cutting Line   •   - · — Joining Line

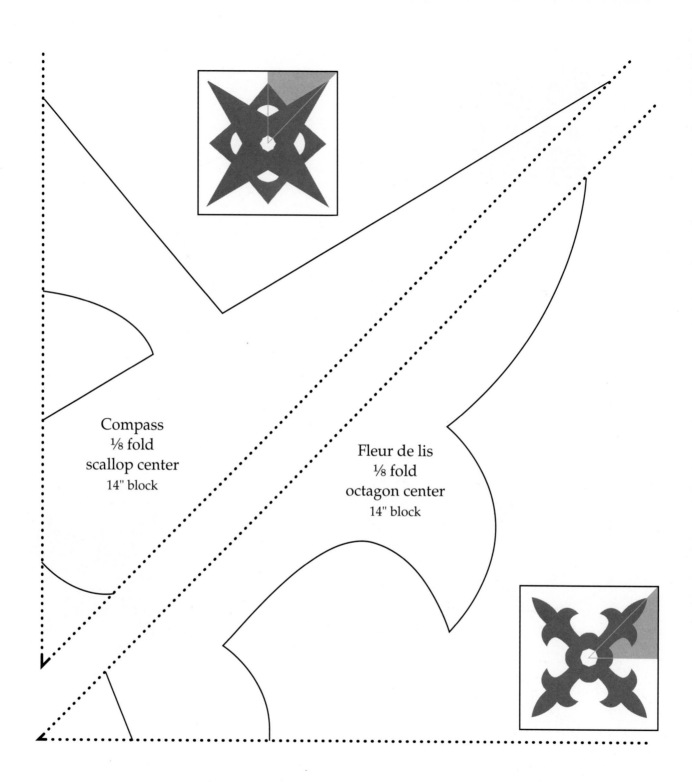

Compass
⅛ fold
scallop center
14" block

Fleur de lis
⅛ fold
octagon center
14" block

· · · · Fold Line   •   - - - Quilting Line   •   —— Cutting Line   •   -·-·— Joining Line

CUTWORK APPLIQUÉ

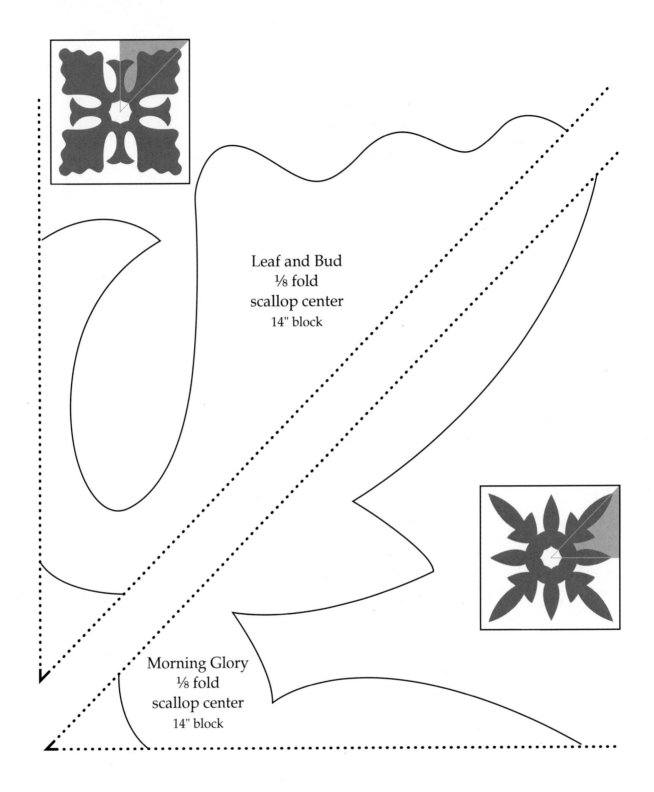

Leaf and Bud
⅛ fold
scallop center
14" block

Morning Glory
⅛ fold
scallop center
14" block

· · · · Fold Line • - - - Quilting Line • ——— Cutting Line • -··- Joining Line

Appliqué with Folded Cutwork: Anita Shackelford

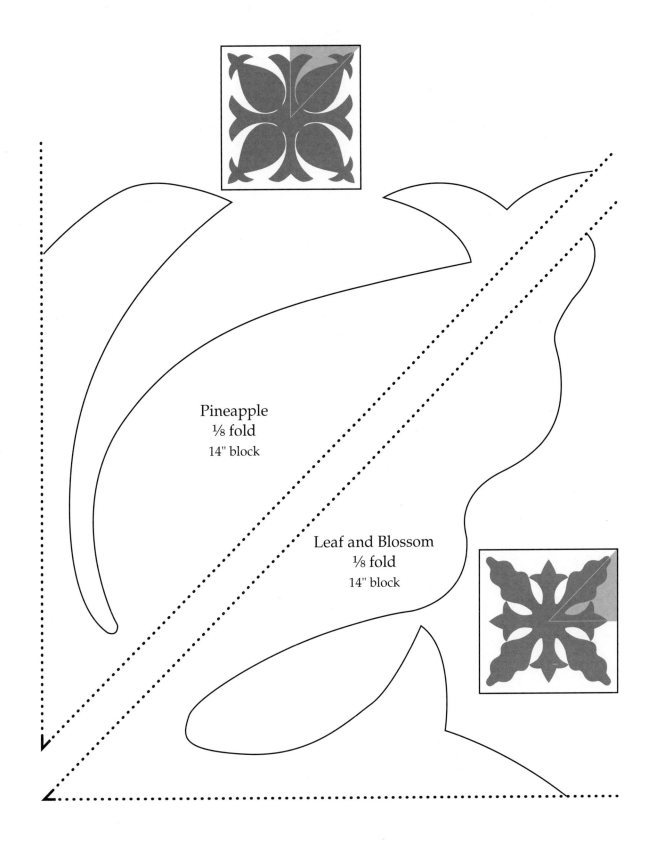

Pineapple
⅛ fold
14" block

Leaf and Blossom
⅛ fold
14" block

· · · · Fold Line • - - - Quilting Line • —— Cutting Line • -·-— Joining Line

CUTWORK APPLIQUÉ

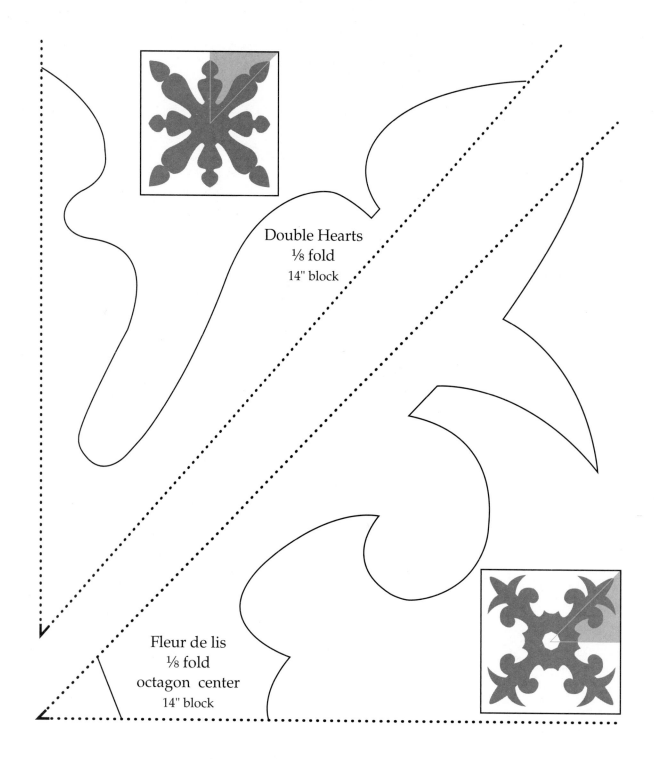

Double Hearts
⅛ fold
14" block

Fleur de lis
⅛ fold
octagon center
14" block

· · · · Fold Line • - - - Quilting Line • —— Cutting Line • -·-· Joining Line

Appliqué with Folded Cutwork: Anita Shackelford

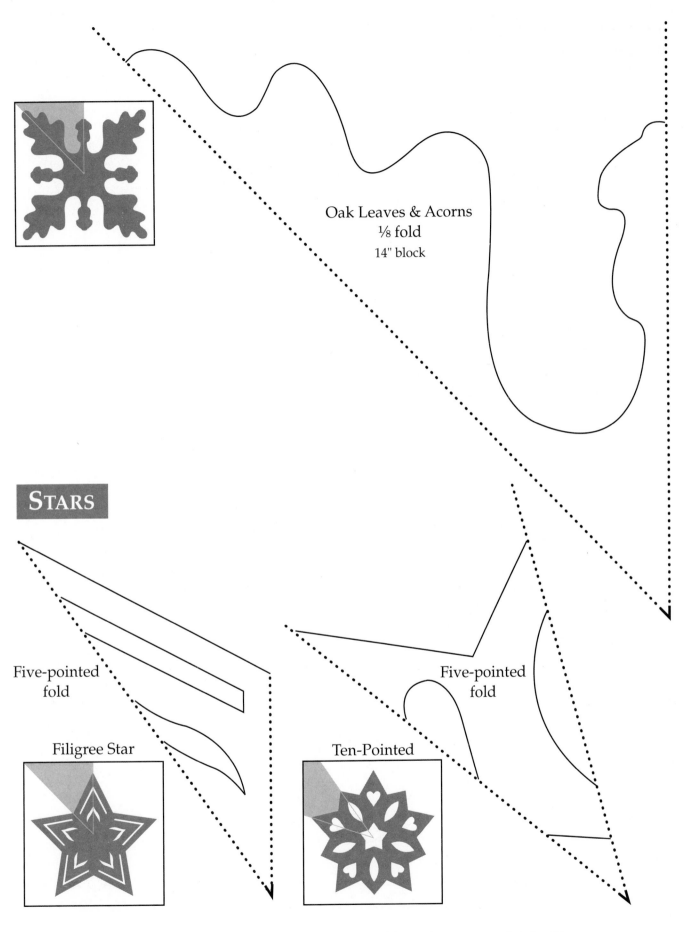

Oak Leaves & Acorns
⅛ fold
14" block

STARS

Five-pointed
fold

Filigree Star

Five-pointed
fold

Ten-Pointed

· · · · Fold Line • - - - Quilting Line • ——— Cutting Line • -·-· Joining Line

SCHERENSCHNITTE

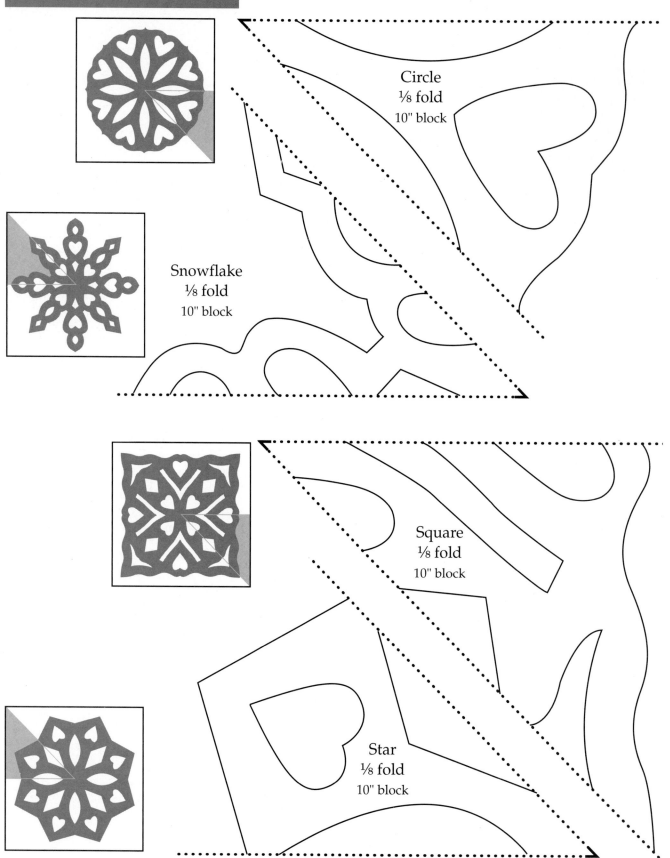

Circle
⅛ fold
10" block

Snowflake
⅛ fold
10" block

Square
⅛ fold
10" block

Star
⅛ fold
10" block

· · · · Fold Line • - - - Quilting Line • —— Cutting Line • -··- Joining Line

Appliqué with Folded Cutwork: Anita Shackelford

¼ fold
10" x 12" block

¼ fold
10" x 12" block

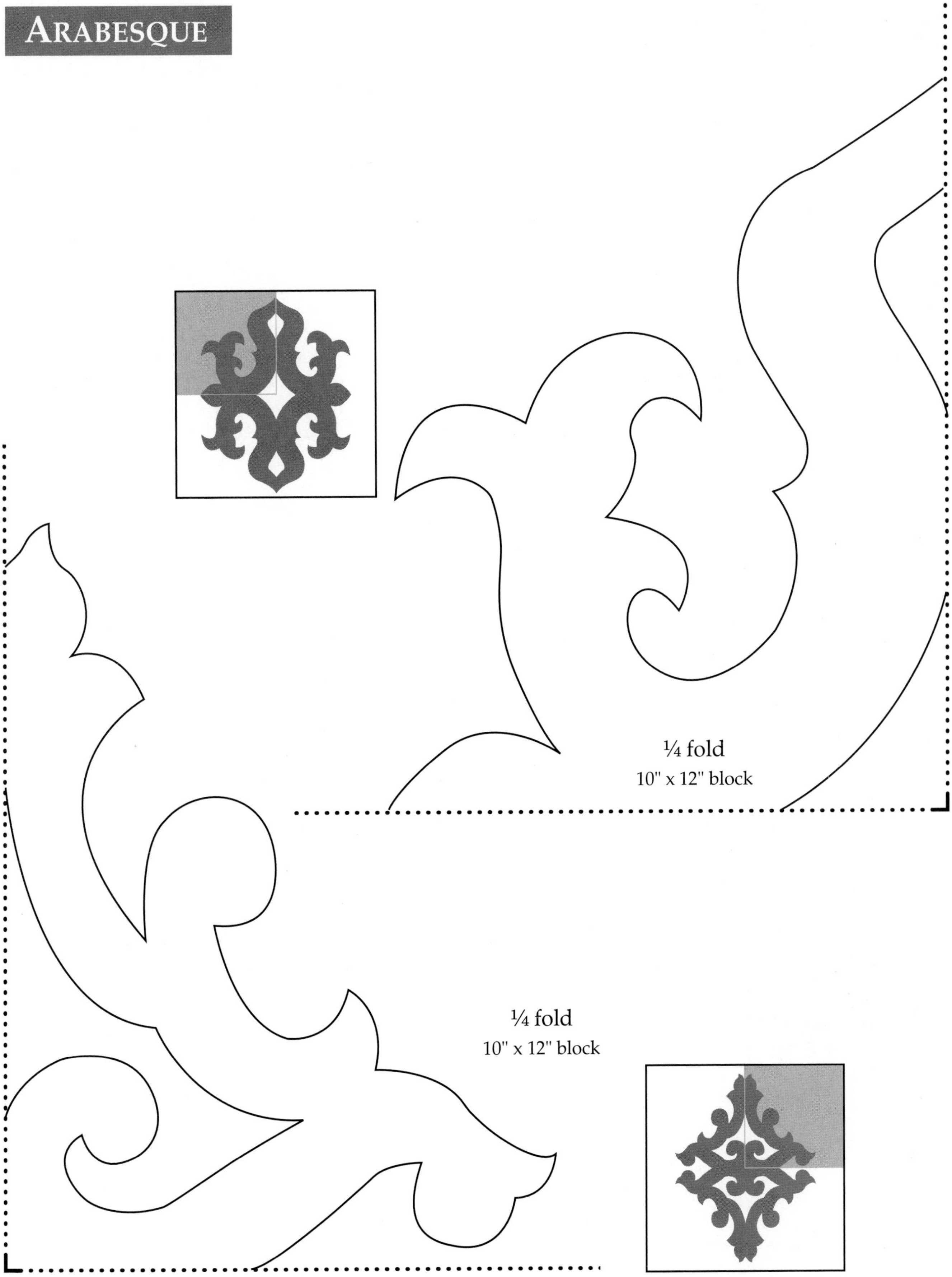

· · · · Fold Line   ·   - - - Quilting Line   ·   —— Cutting Line   ·   -·—· Joining Line

Appliqué with Folded Cutwork: Anita Shackelford

January
⅙ fold
15" block

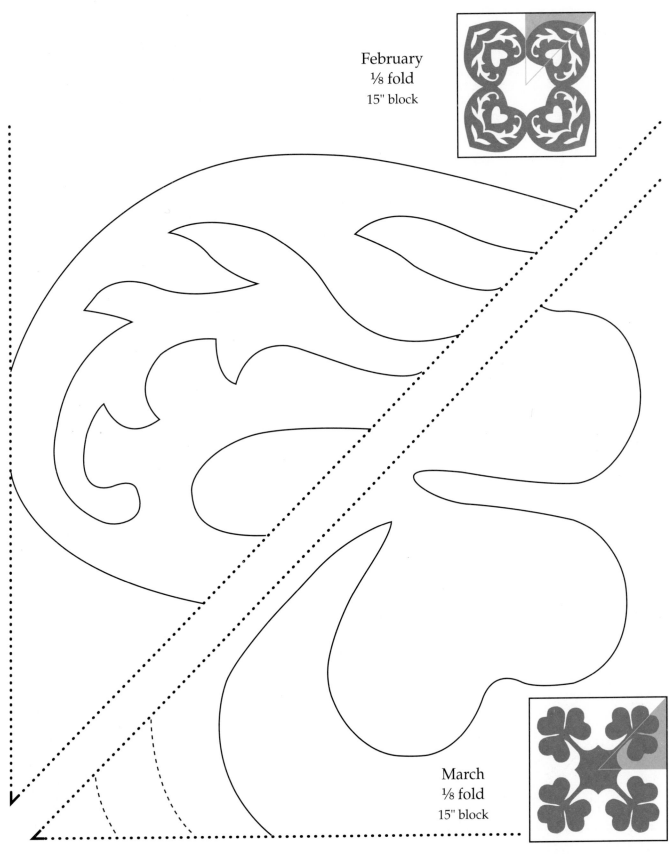

February
⅛ fold
15" block

March
⅛ fold
15" block

· · · · Fold Line • - - - Quilting Line • —— Cutting Line • -·-·- Joining Line

TIMES AND SEASONS

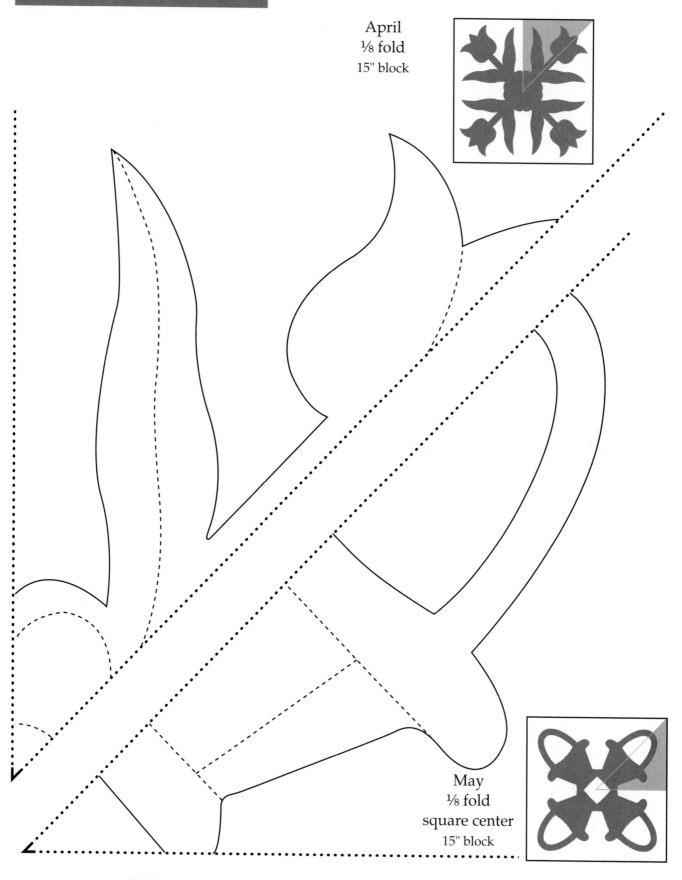

April
⅛ fold
15" block

May
⅛ fold
square center
15" block

· · · · Fold Line • - - - Quilting Line • —— Cutting Line • -·- Joining Line

Appliqué with Folded Cutwork: Anita Shackelford

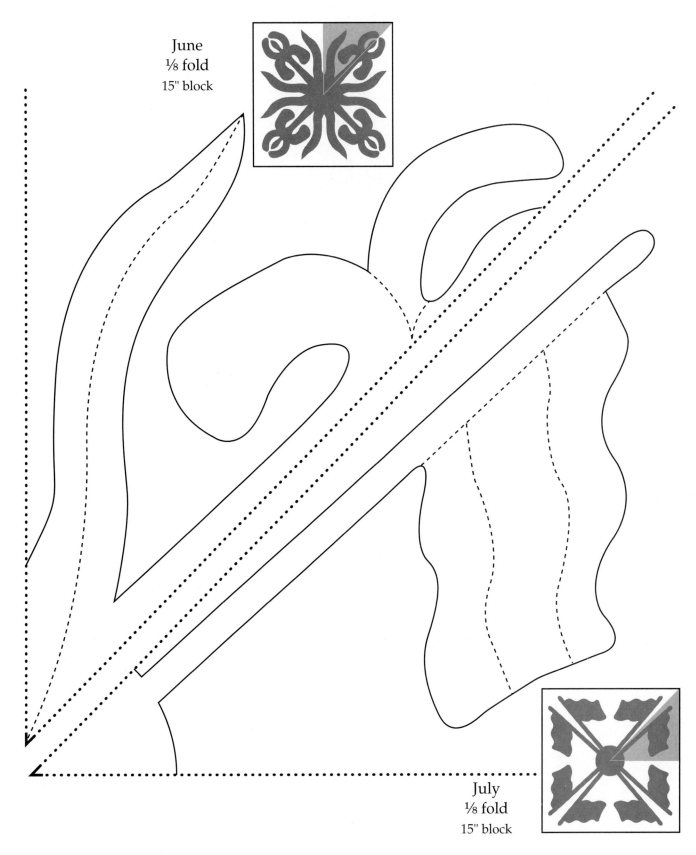

June
⅛ fold
15" block

July
⅛ fold
15" block

· · · · Fold Line • - - - Quilting Line • ——— Cutting Line • -·-· Joining Line

Appliqué with Folded Cutwork: Anita Shackelford

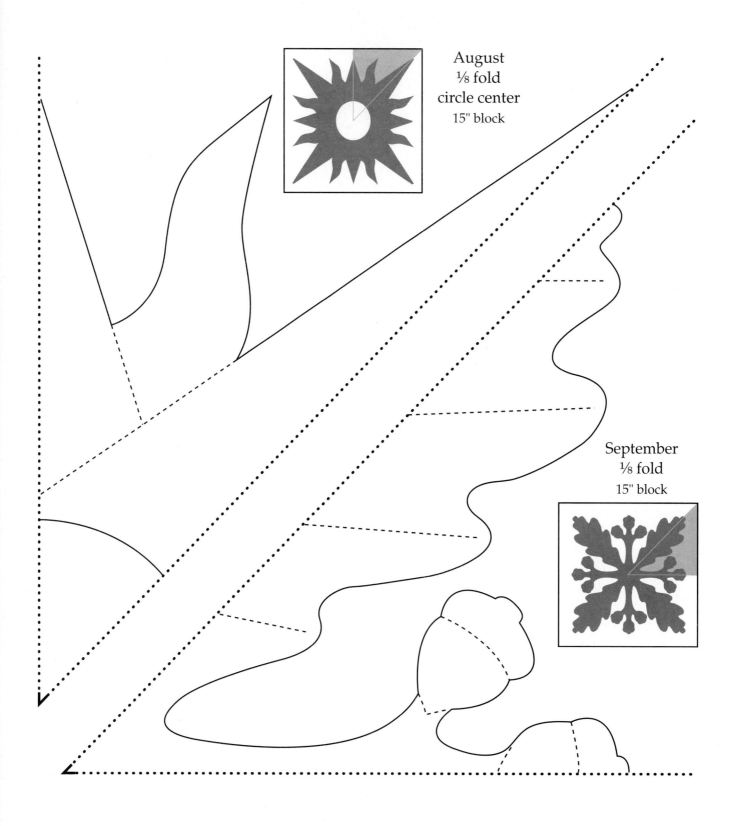

August
⅛ fold
circle center
15" block

September
⅛ fold
15" block

· · · · Fold Line • - - - Quilting Line • —— Cutting Line • -··- Joining Line

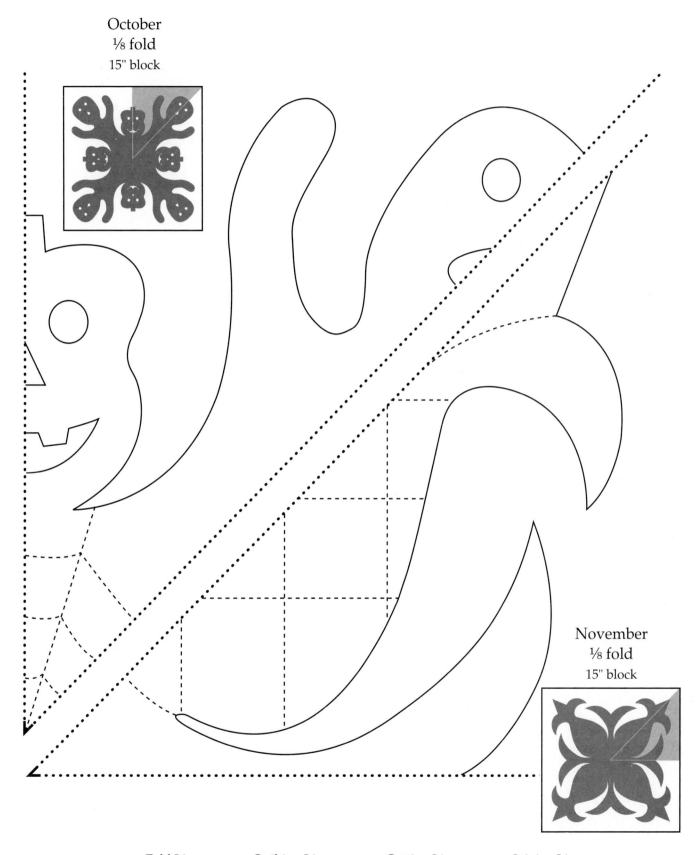

For felt and straight stitch appliqué, shown on p. 77, photocopy at 133% for 20" blocks.

October
⅛ fold
15" block

November
⅛ fold
15" block

· · · · Fold Line • - - - Quilting Line • —— Cutting Line • -·-·— Joining Line

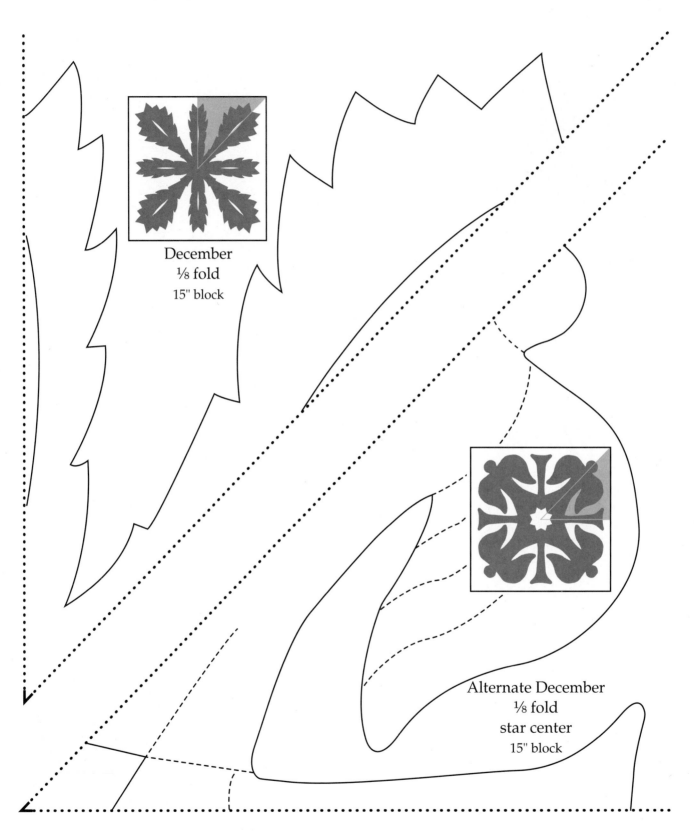

December
⅛ fold
15" block

Alternate December
⅛ fold
star center
15" block

· · · · Fold Line • - - - Quilting Line • —— Cutting Line • -·-· Joining Line

Appliqué with Folded Cutwork: Anita Shackelford

LAYERED DESERT SENTINEL

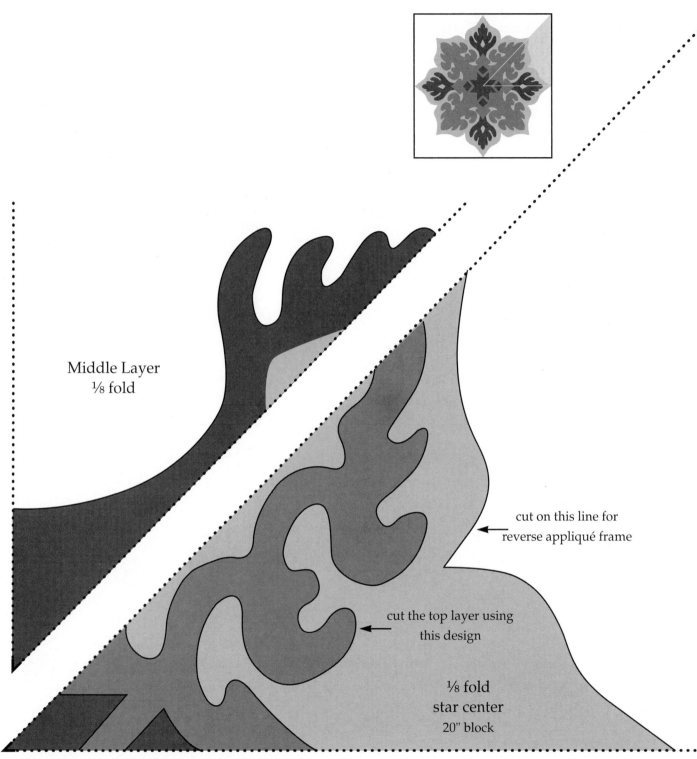

Middle Layer
⅛ fold

cut on this line for
reverse appliqué frame

cut the top layer using
this design

⅛ fold
star center
20" block

· · · · Fold Line • - - - Quilting Line • —— Cutting Line • -··- Joining Line

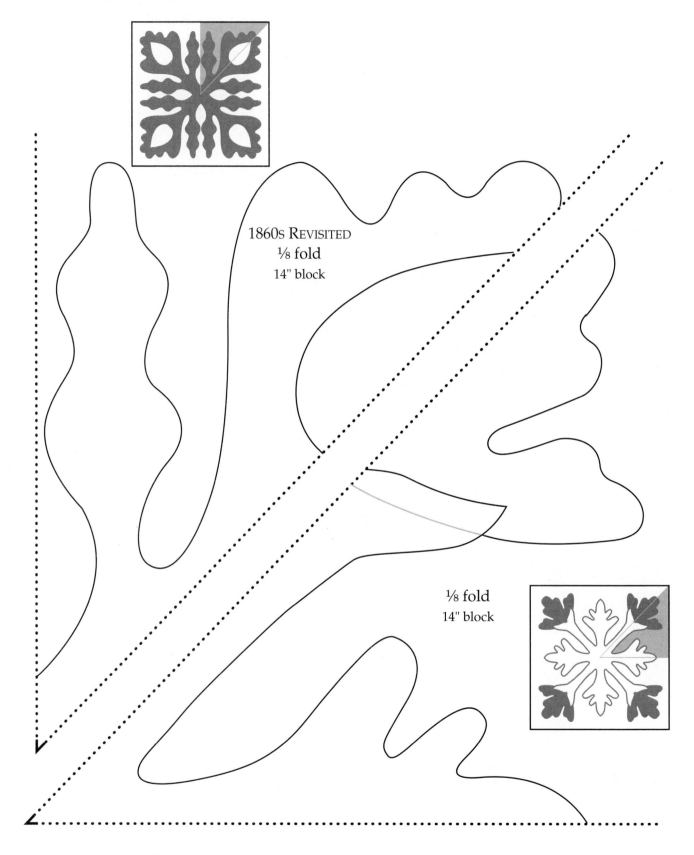

1860s REVISITED
⅛ fold
14" block

⅛ fold
14" block

· · · · Fold Line   •   - - - Quilting Line   •   —— Cutting Line   •   -··— Joining Line

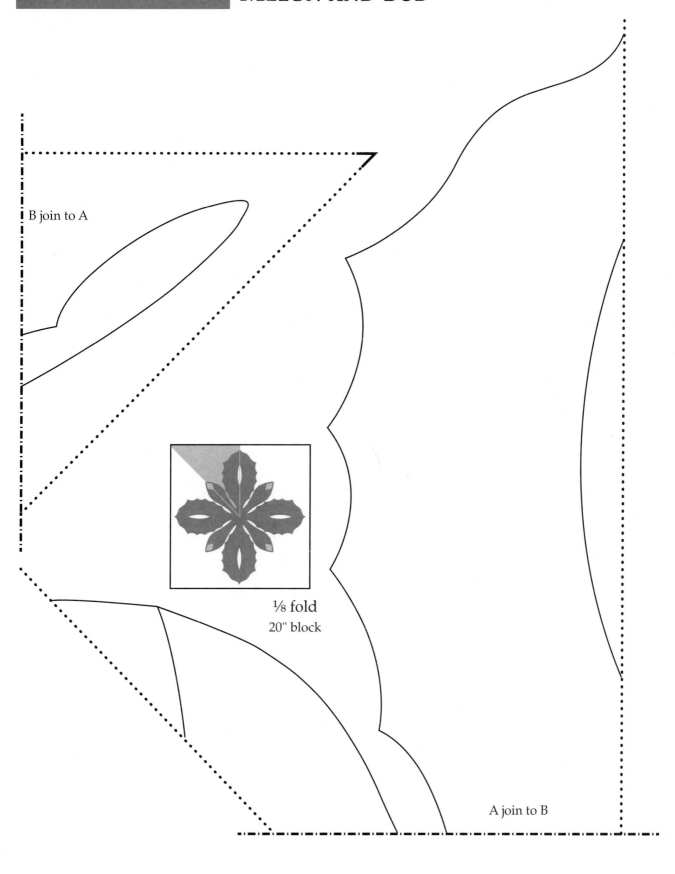

B join to A

¹/₈ fold
20" block

A join to B

········ Fold Line   • - - - Quilting Line   • ——— Cutting Line   • -·-·- Joining Line

Four Seasons **Embellished**

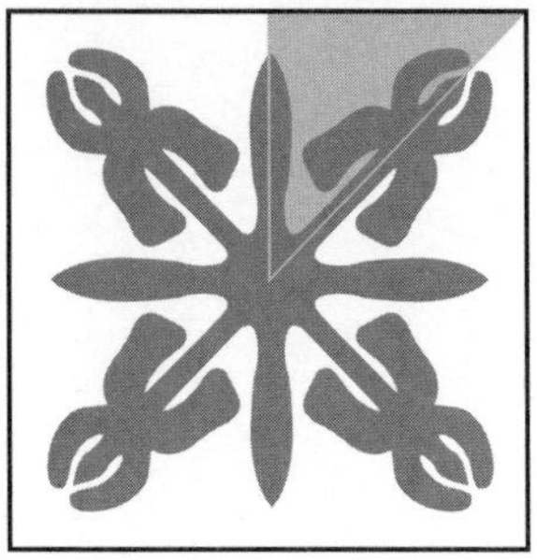

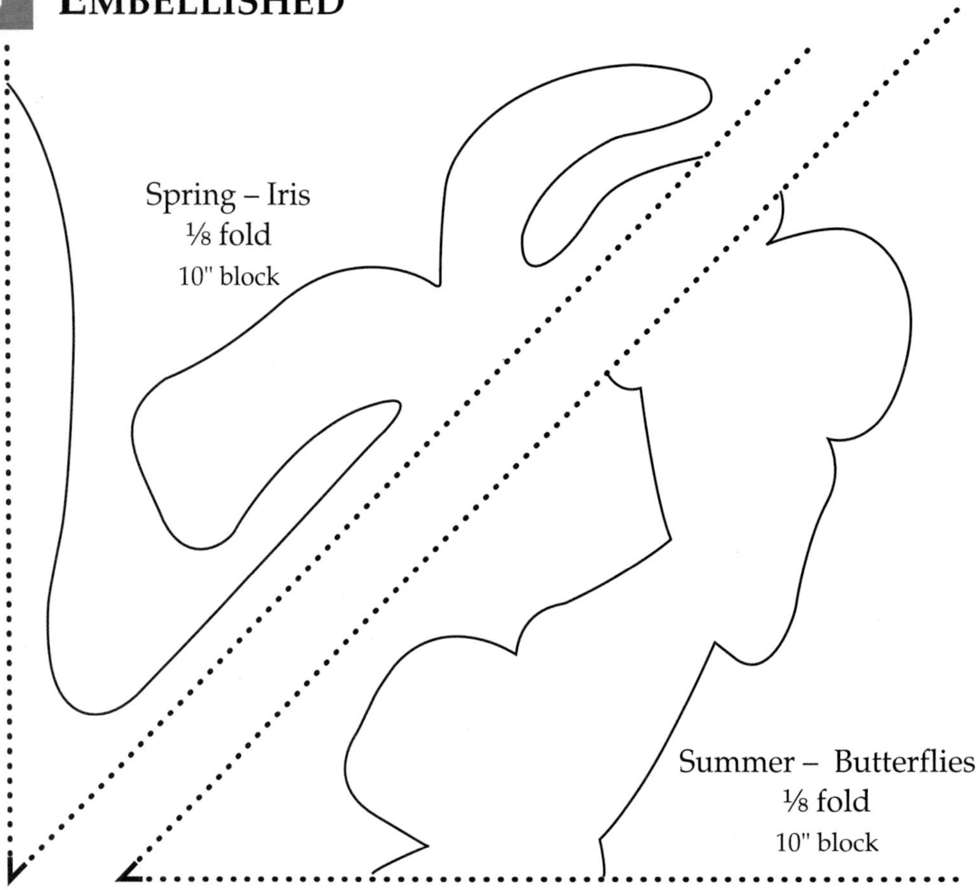
Spring – Iris
⅛ fold
10" block
Summer – Butterflies
⅛ fold
10" block

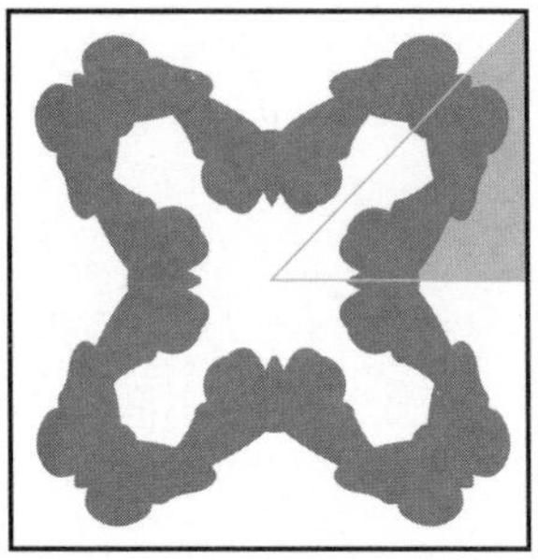

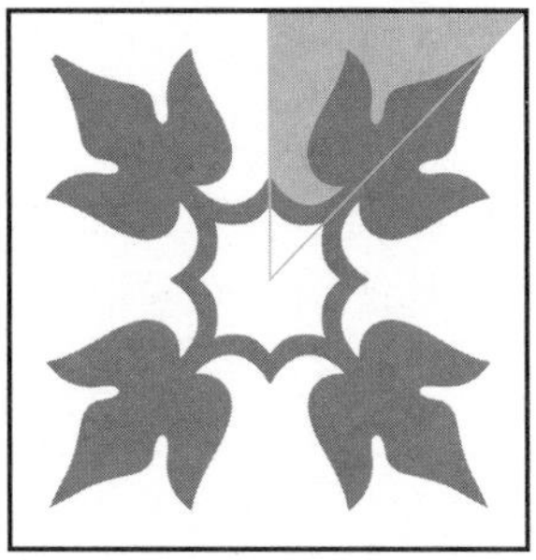

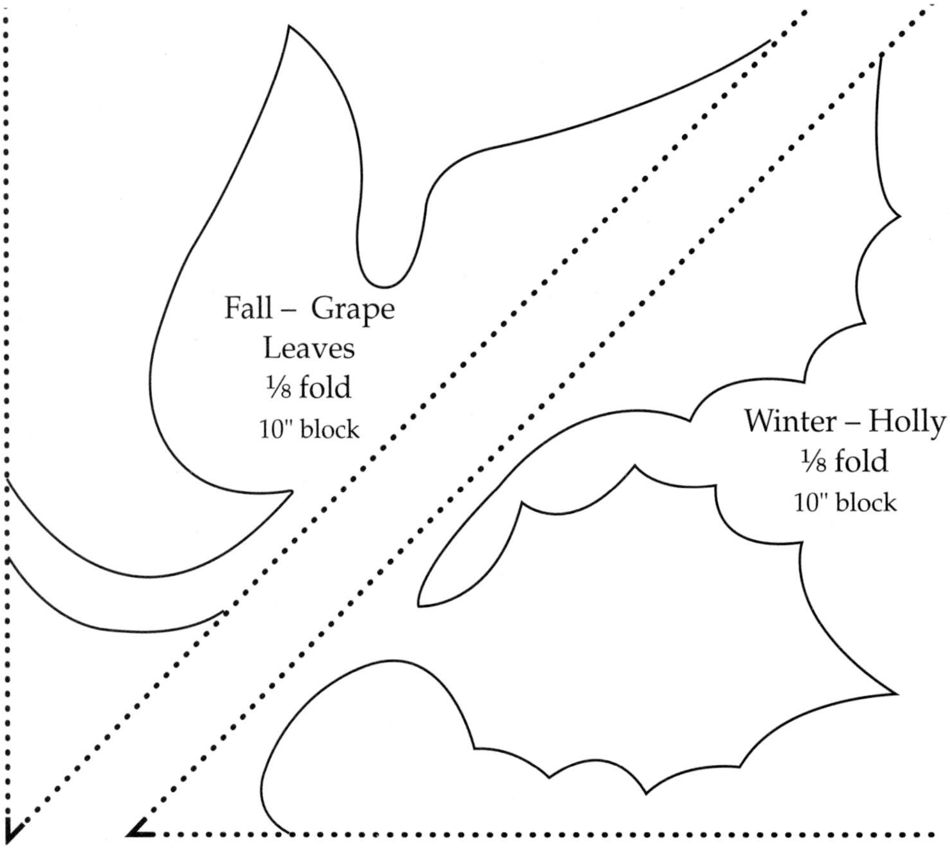
Fall – Grape
Leaves
⅛ fold
10" block
Winter – Holly
⅛ fold
10" block

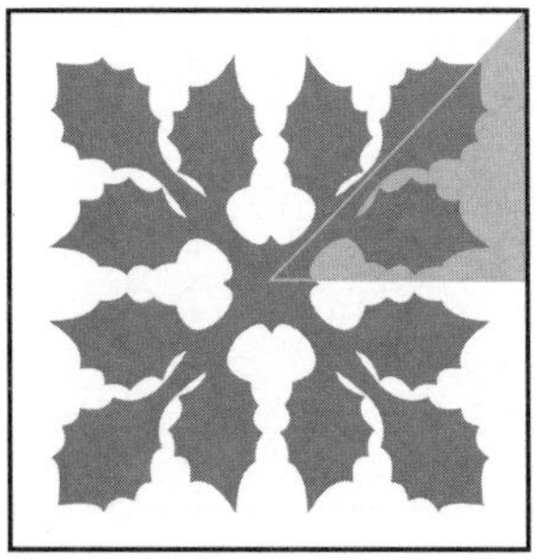

· · · · Fold Line • - - - Quilting Line • —— Cutting Line • -·— Joining Line

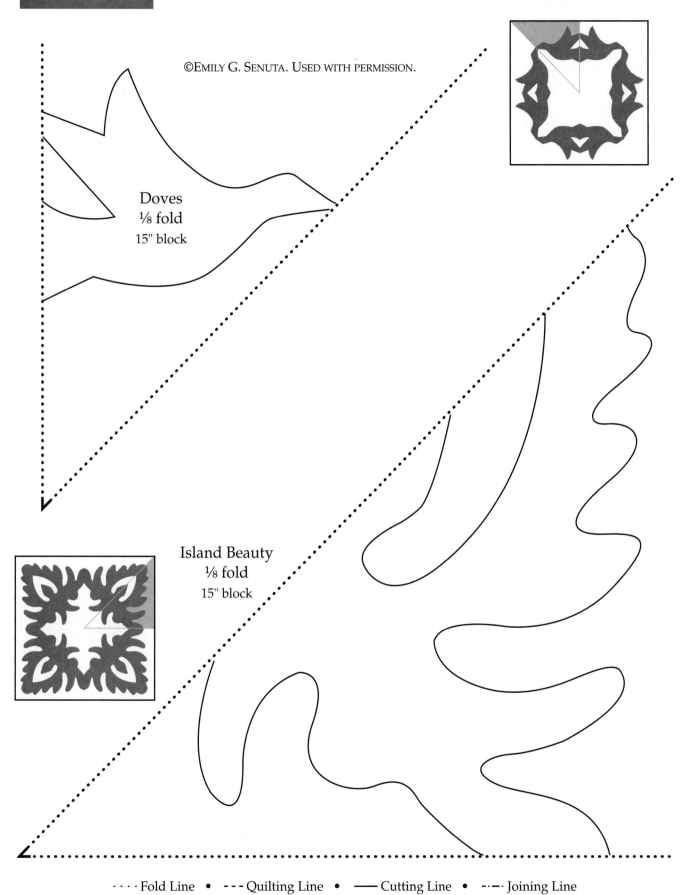

WREATHS

©Emily G. Senuta. Used with permission.

Doves
⅛ fold
15" block

Island Beauty
⅛ fold
15" block

· · · · Fold Line • - - - Quilting Line • —— Cutting Line • -·-· Joining Line

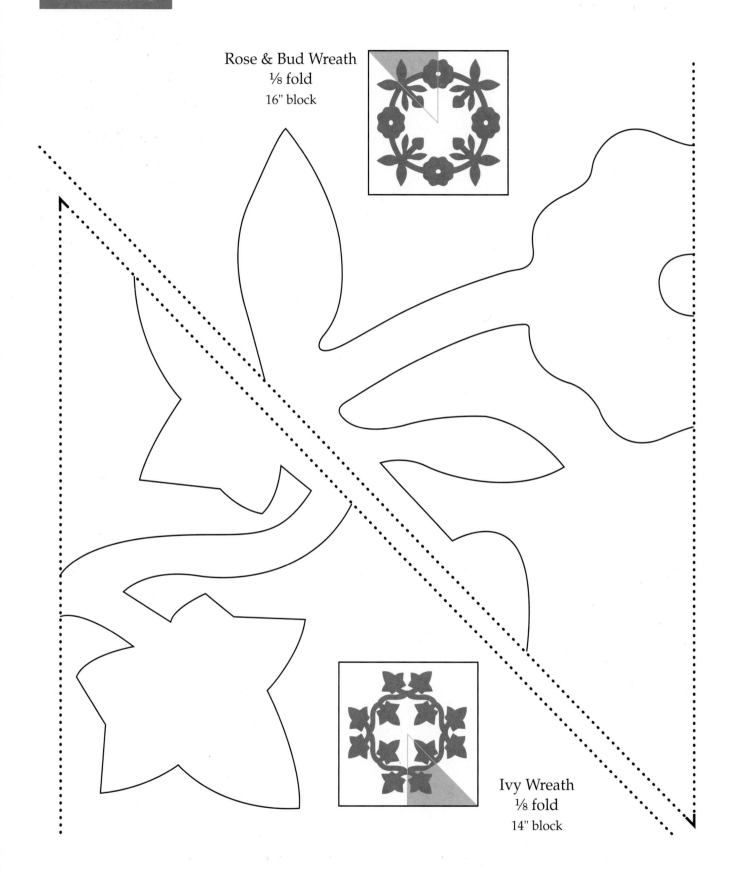

Rose & Bud Wreath
⅛ fold
16" block

Ivy Wreath
⅛ fold
14" block

· · · · Fold Line · - - - Quilting Line · —— Cutting Line · -·- Joining Line

Appliqué with Folded Cutwork: Anita Shackelford

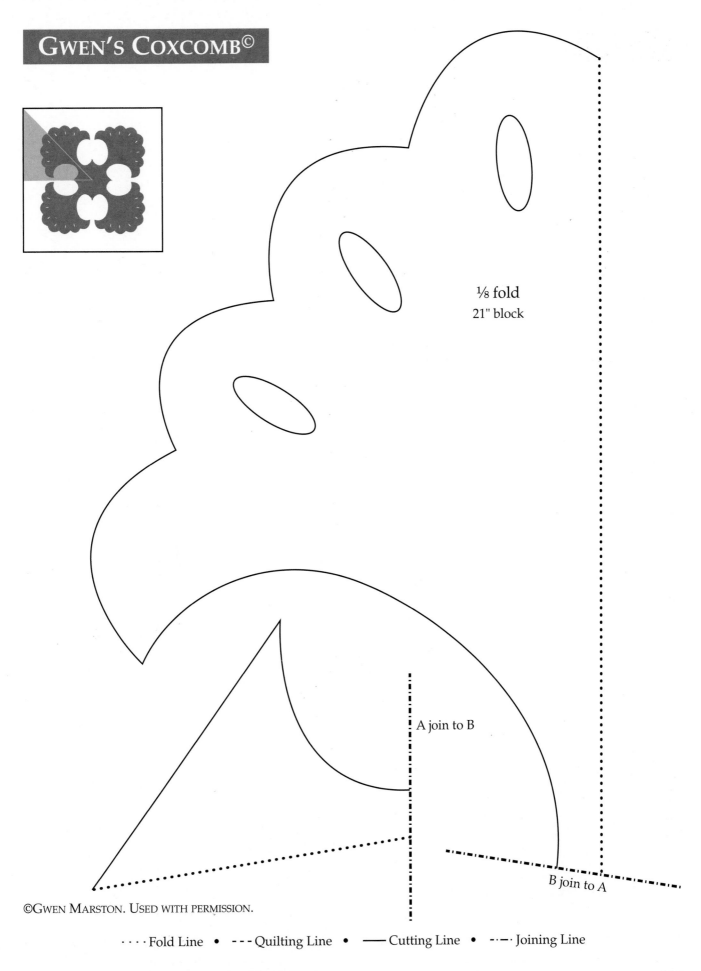

GWEN'S COXCOMB©

⅛ fold
21" block

A join to B

B join to A

· · · · Fold Line   • - - - Quilting Line   • ——— Cutting Line   • —·— Joining Line

Appliqué with Folded Cutwork: Anita Shackelford

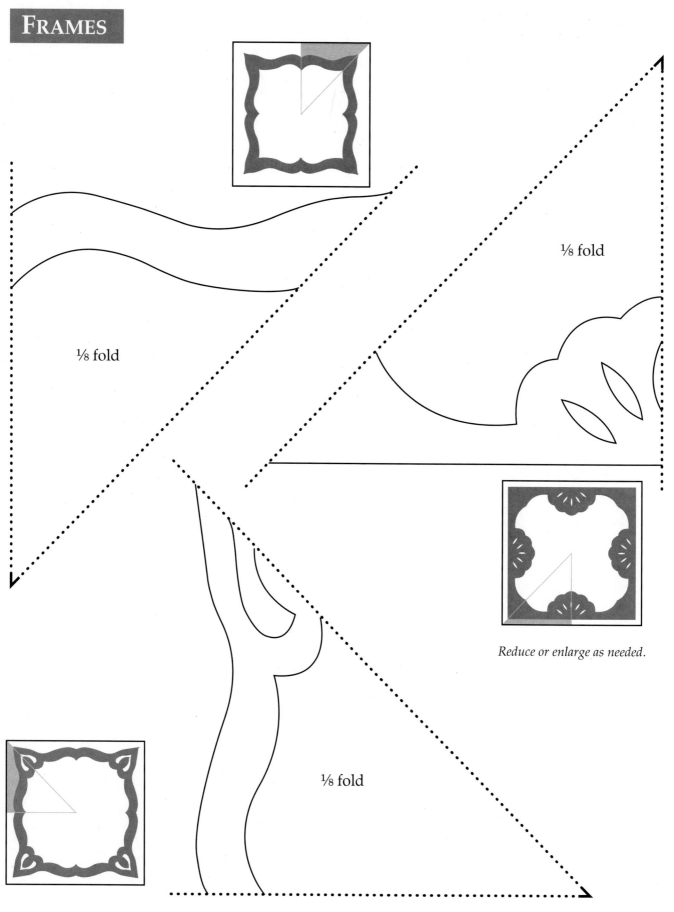

⅛ fold

⅛ fold

⅛ fold

⅛ fold

Reduce or enlarge as needed.

· · · · Fold Line • - - - Quilting Line • —— Cutting Line • -·-· Joining Line

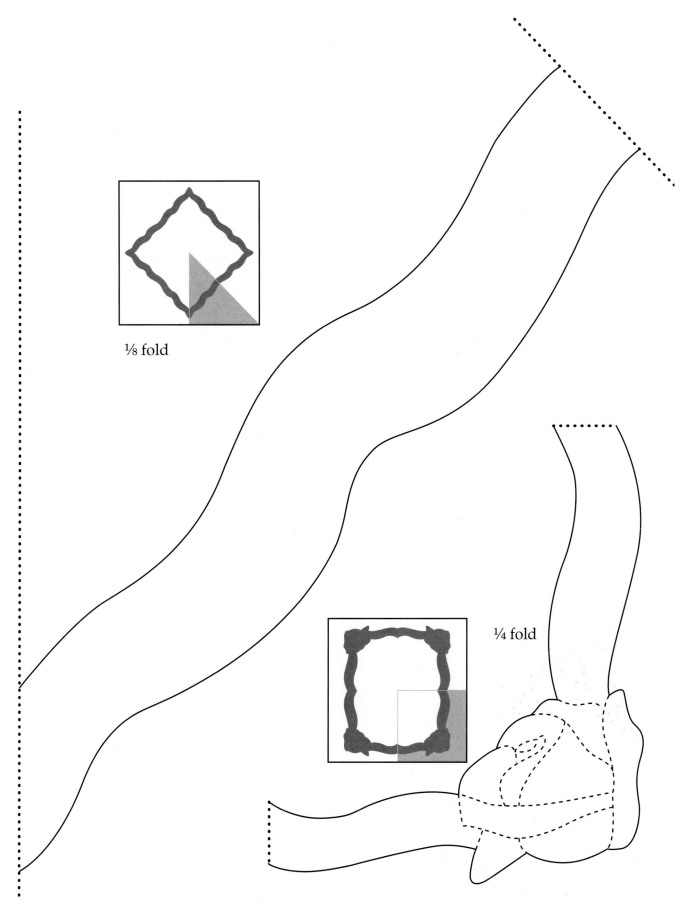

⅛ fold

¼ fold

· · · Fold Line　•　- - - Quilting Line　•　——— Cutting Line　•　-·- Joining Line

Friendship Album

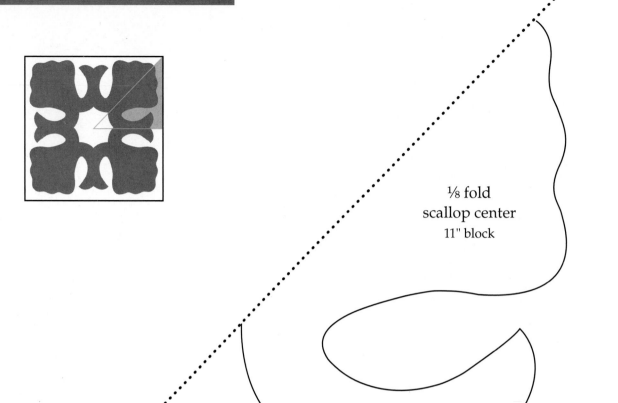

⅛ fold
scallop center
11" block

Oak and Acorn

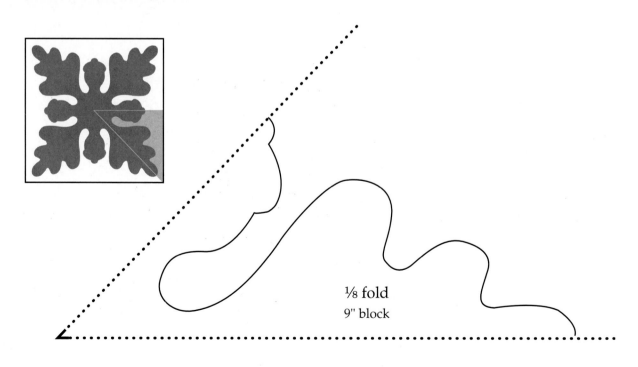

⅛ fold
9" block

· · · · Fold Line • - - - Quilting Line • —— Cutting Line • -·-· Joining Line

Appliqué with Folded Cutwork: Anita Shackelford

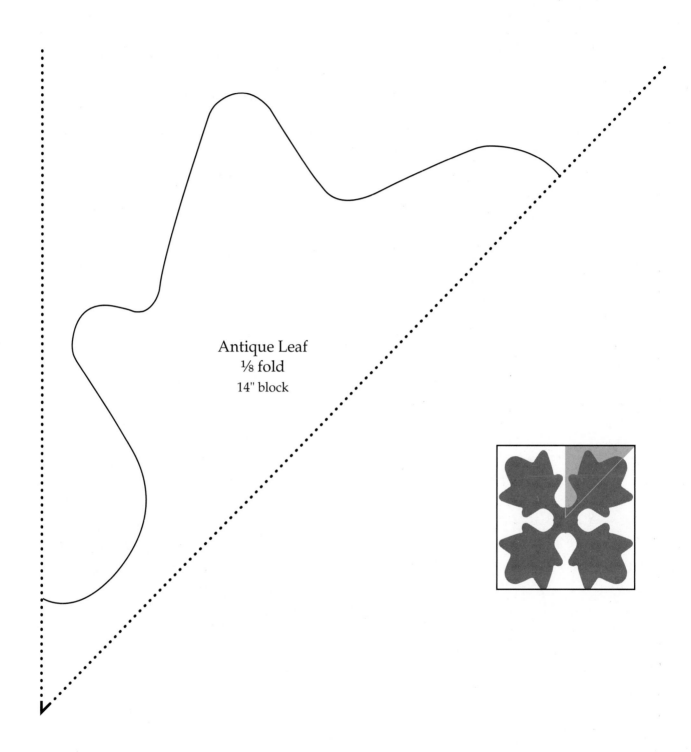

Antique Leaf
⅛ fold
14" block

· · · · Fold Line   •   - - - Quilting Line   •   —— Cutting Line   •   -··- Joining Line

Hawaiian Four Block

Enlarge these designs 133% for 20" blocks.

⅛ fold
15" block

· · · · Fold Line　·　- - - Quilting Line　·　—— Cutting Line　·　-·-· Joining Line

Appliqué with Folded Cutwork: Anita Shackelford

⅛ fold
15" block

· · · · Fold Line • - - - Quilting Line • —— Cutting Line • -·-· Joining Line

Appliqué with Folded Cutwork: Anita Shackelford

HAWAIIAN FOUR BLOCK

Enlarge these designs 133% for 20" blocks.

⅛ fold
15" block

· · · · Fold Line   •   - - - Quilting Line   •   —— Cutting Line   •   -··- Joining Line

Appliqué with Folded Cutwork: Anita Shackelford

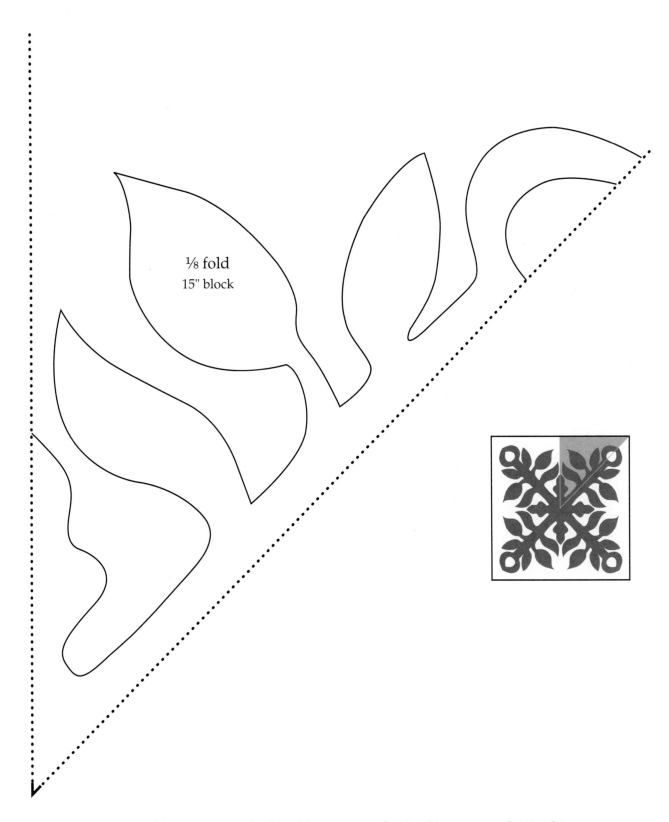

⅛ fold
15" block

···· Fold Line • ---- Quilting Line • —— Cutting Line • -·-· Joining Line

KANGAROO

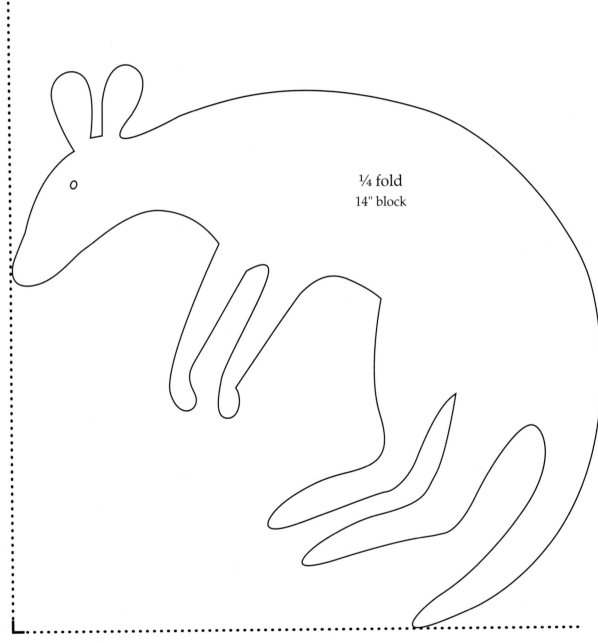

¼ fold
14" block

· · · · Fold Line   •   - - - Quilting Line   •   —— Cutting Line   •   -·- Joining Line

Appliqué with Folded Cutwork: Anita Shackelford

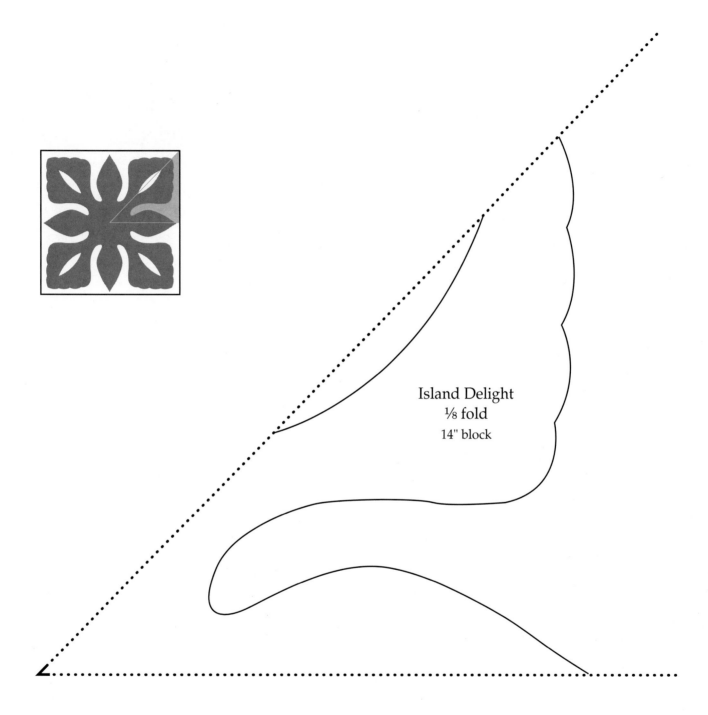

Island Delight
⅛ fold
14" block

· · · · Fold Line • - - - Quilting Line • —— Cutting Line • -·- Joining Line

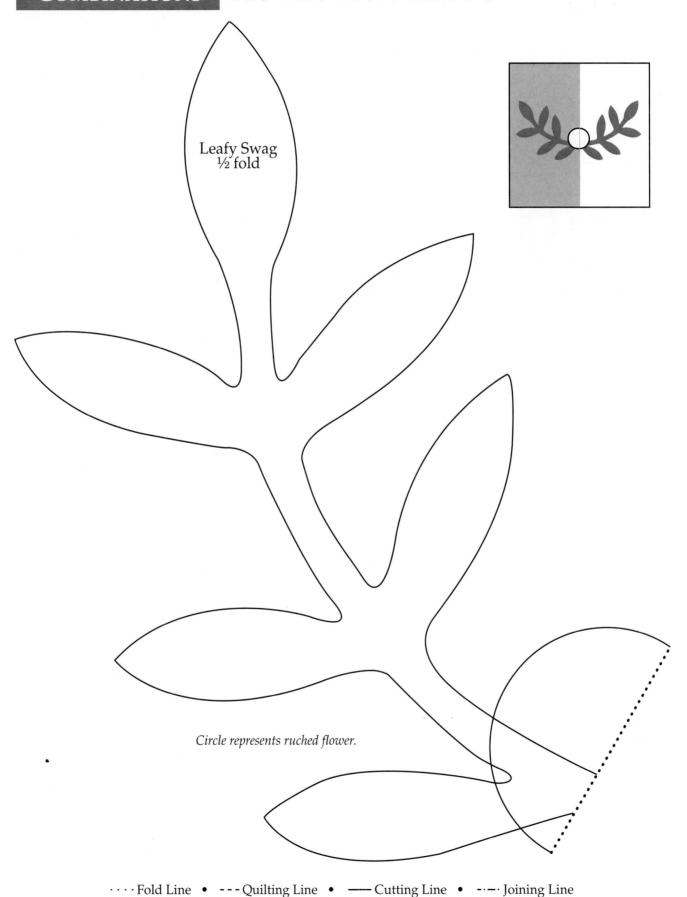

Leafy Swag
½ fold

Circle represents ruched flower.

· · · · Fold Line   •   - - - Quilting Line   •   ——— Cutting Line   •   - · - Joining Line

Appliqué with Folded Cutwork: Anita Shackelford

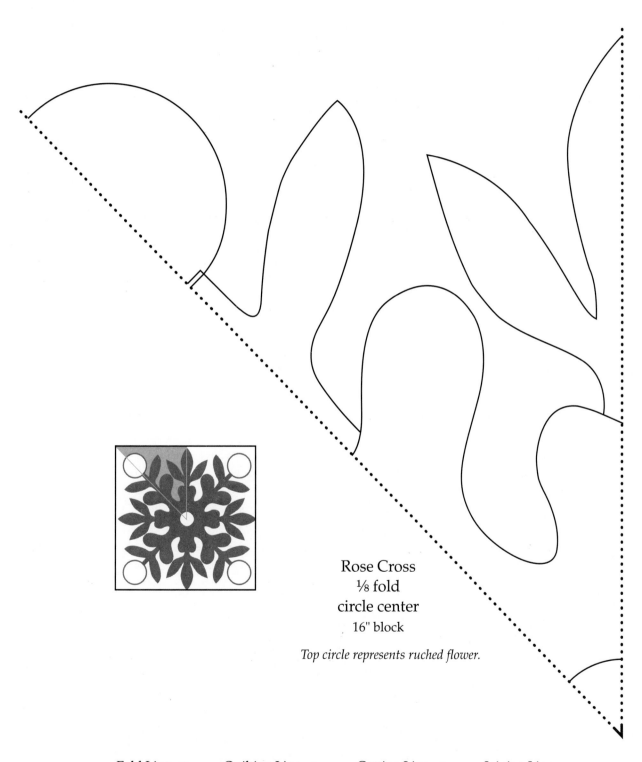

Rose Cross
⅛ fold
circle center
16" block

Top circle represents ruched flower.

· · · · Fold Line • - - - Quilting Line • —— Cutting Line • -·-· Joining Line

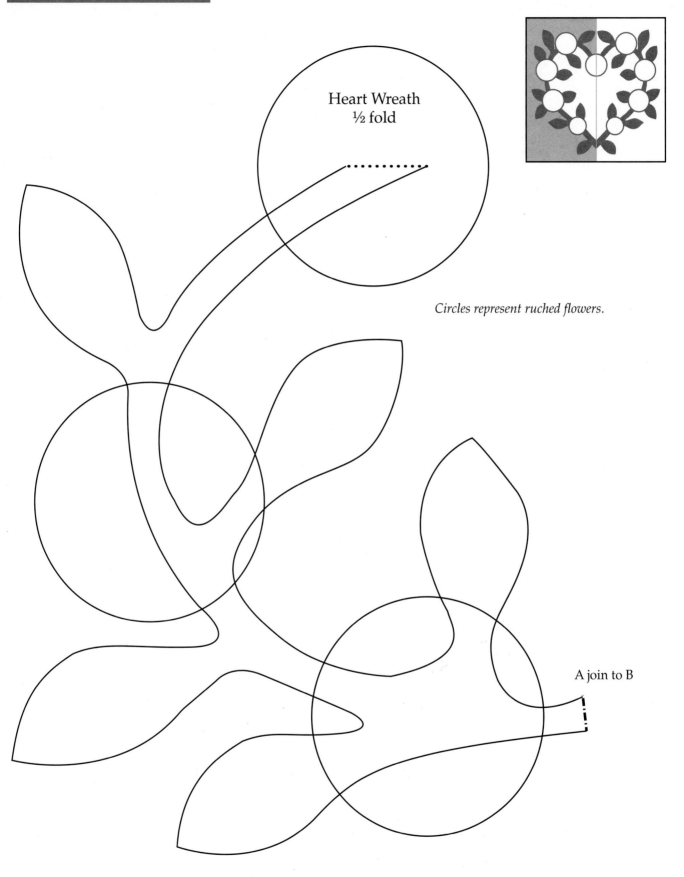

Heart Wreath
½ fold

Circles represent ruched flowers.

A join to B

· · · · Fold Line • - - - Quilting Line • —— Cutting Line • -·-— Joining Line

Appliqué with Folded Cutwork: Anita Shackelford

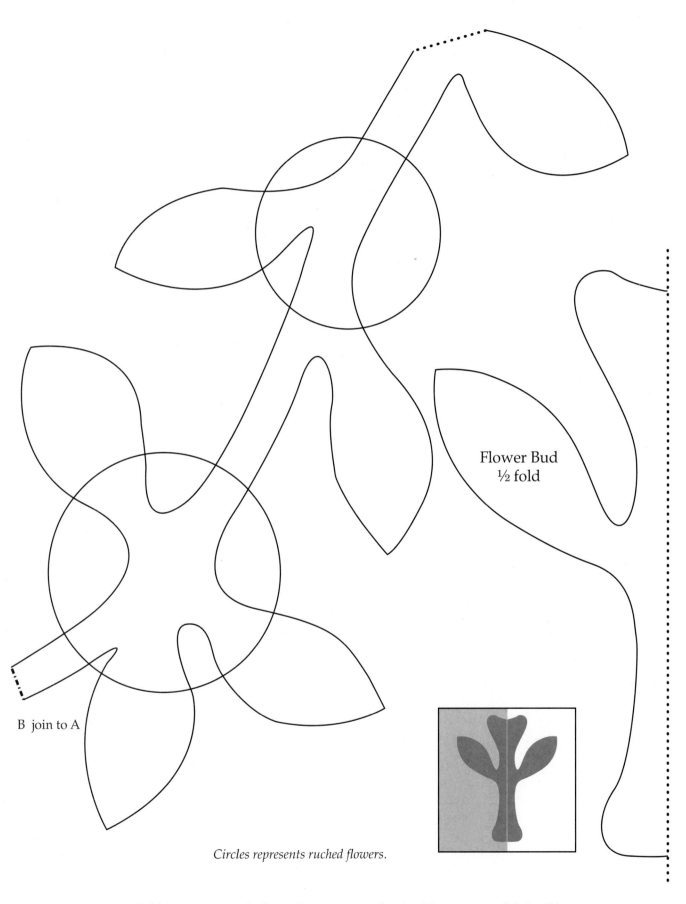

Flower Bud
½ fold

B join to A

Circles represents ruched flowers.

· · · · Fold Line • - - - Quilting Line • —— Cutting Line • -·-· Joining Line

FLOWERS FROM FRIENDS

Lyre
½ fold
16" block

A join to B

16" block

Circles represent ruched flowers.

· · · · Fold Line • - - - Quilting Line • —— Cutting Line • -·-· Joining Line

Appliqué with Folded Cutwork: Anita Shackelford

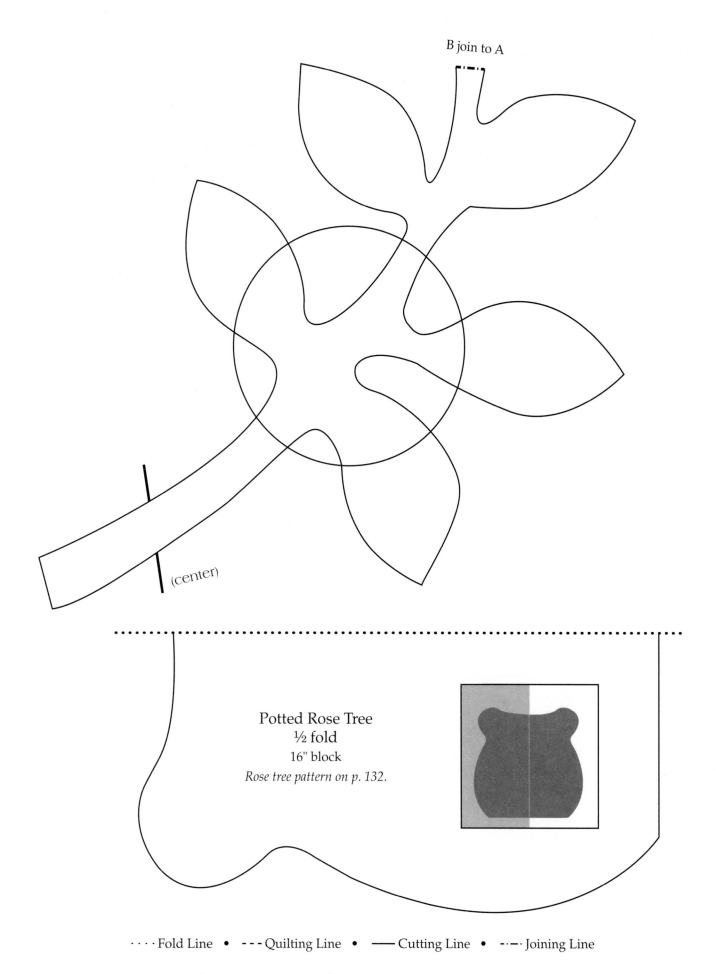

B join to A

(center)

Potted Rose Tree
½ fold
16" block
Rose tree pattern on p. 132.

· · · · Fold Line   •   - - - Quilting Line   •   —— Cutting Line   •   -·-· Joining Line

FLOWERS FROM FRIENDS

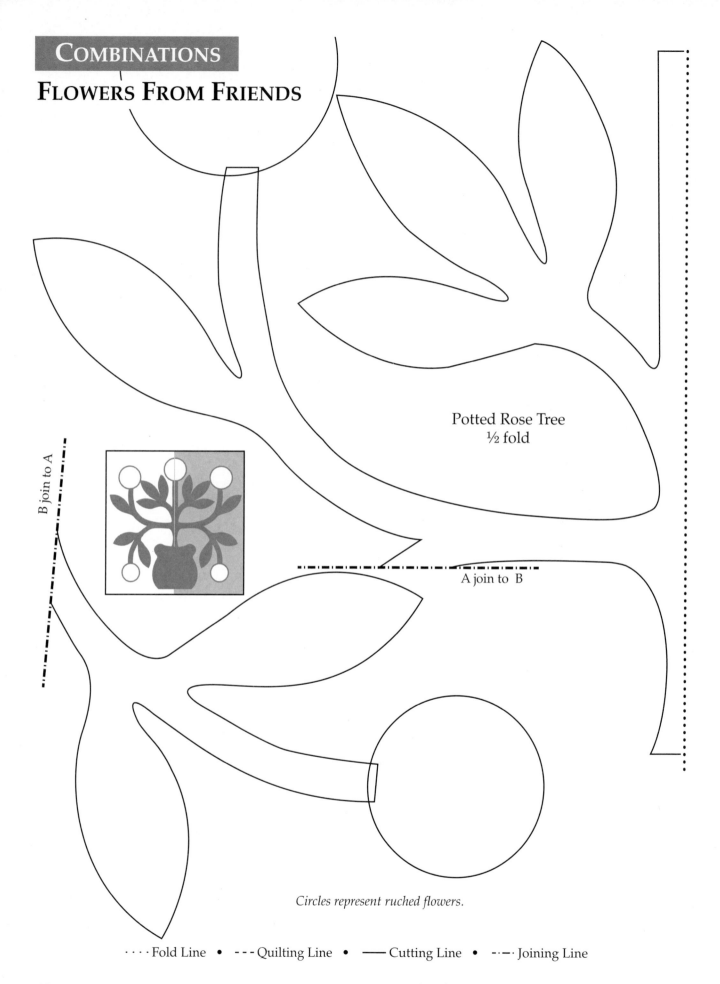

Potted Rose Tree
½ fold

B join to A

A join to B

Circles represent ruched flowers.

· · · · Fold Line • - - - Quilting Line • —— Cutting Line • -·— Joining Line

Appliqué with Folded Cutwork: Anita Shackelford

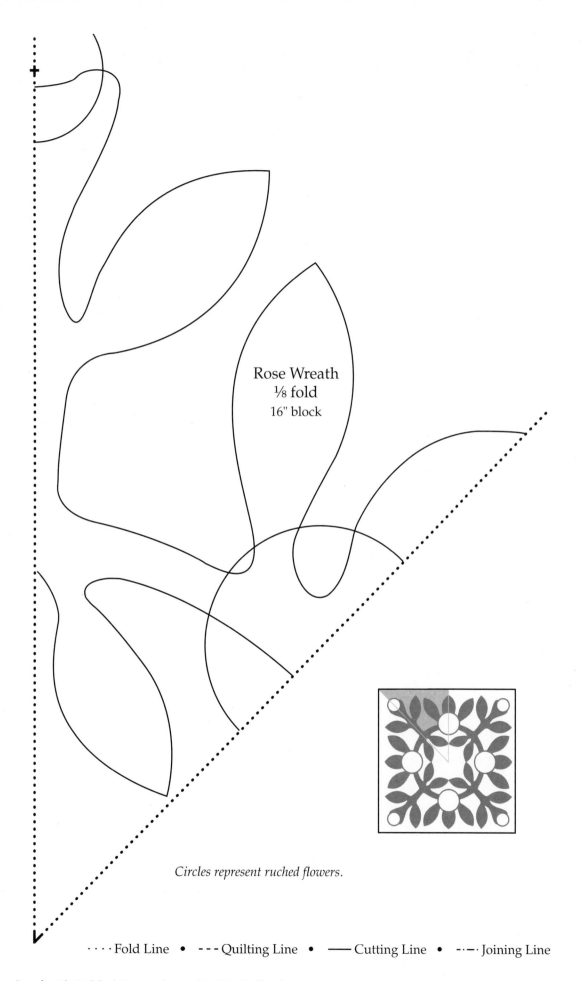

Rose Wreath
⅛ fold
16" block

Circles represent ruched flowers.

····Fold Line • ---Quilting Line • ——Cutting Line • -··—Joining Line

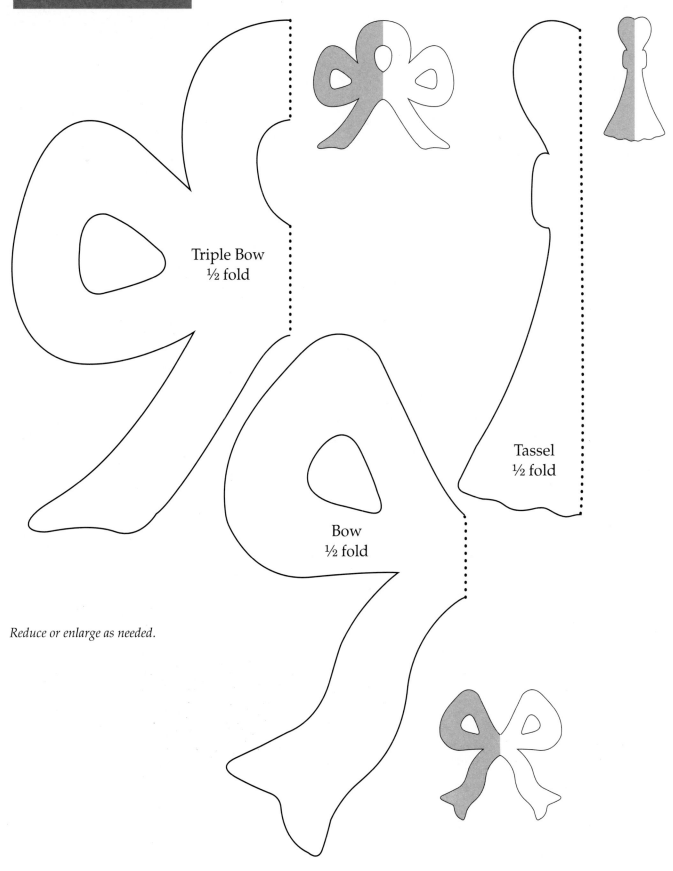

Triple Bow
½ fold

Tassel
½ fold

Bow
½ fold

Reduce or enlarge as needed.

· · · · Fold Line   •   - - - Quilting Line   •   —— Cutting Line   •   -·— Joining Line

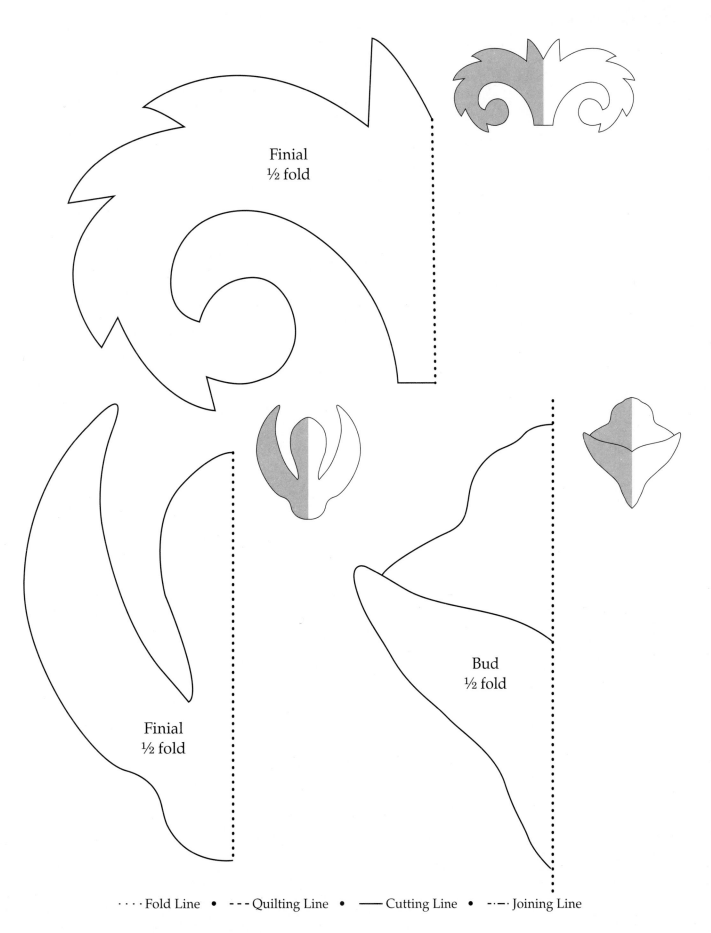

Finial
½ fold

Finial
½ fold

Bud
½ fold

· · · · Fold Line   •   - - - Quilting Line   •   —— Cutting Line   •   —·— Joining Line

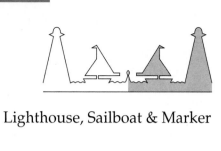

Lighthouse, Sailboat & Marker

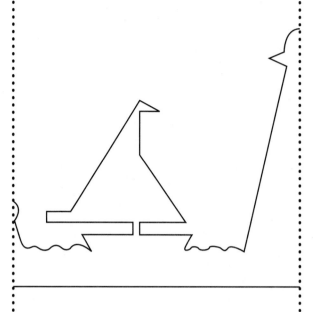

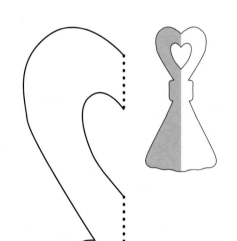

Reduce or enlarge as needed.

Dog & Tree

Tassel
½ fold

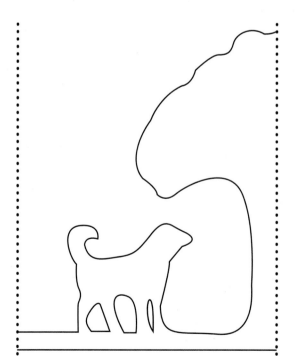

· · · · Fold Line • - - - Quilting Line • —— Cutting Line • -·-· Joining Line

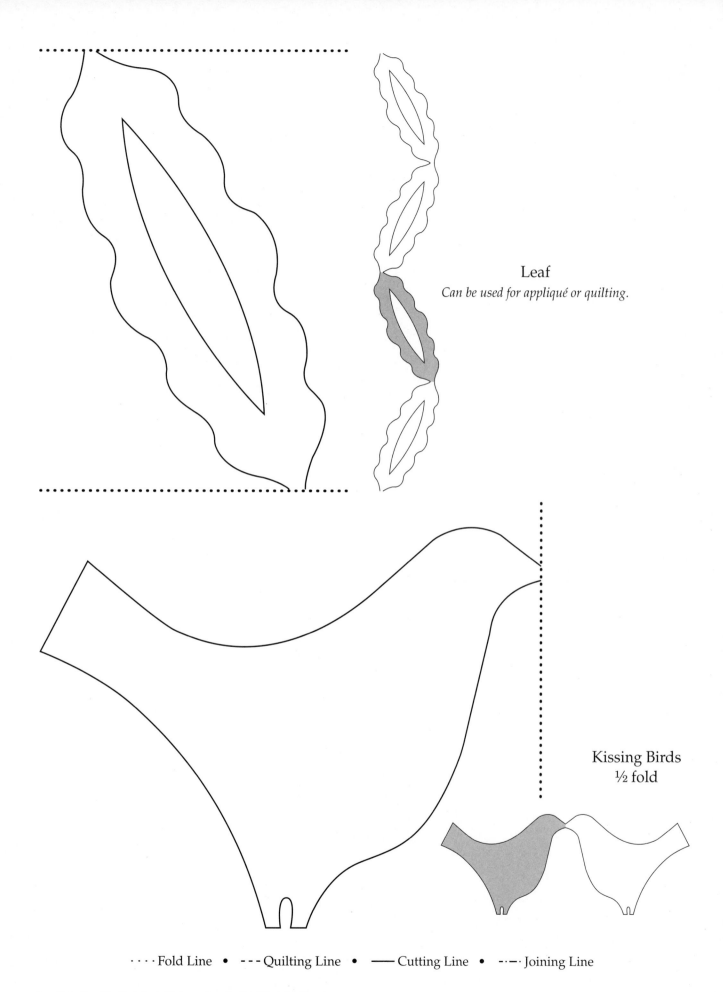

Leaf

Can be used for appliqué or quilting.

Kissing Birds
½ fold

· · · Fold Line • - - - Quilting Line • —— Cutting Line • -·-· Joining Line

Appliqué with Folded Cutwork: Anita Shackelford

Oak and Spruce

Liberty Tree

· · · · Fold Line   •   - - - Quilting Line   •   —— Cutting Line   •   -··— Joining Line

Appliqué with Folded Cutwork: Anita Shackelford

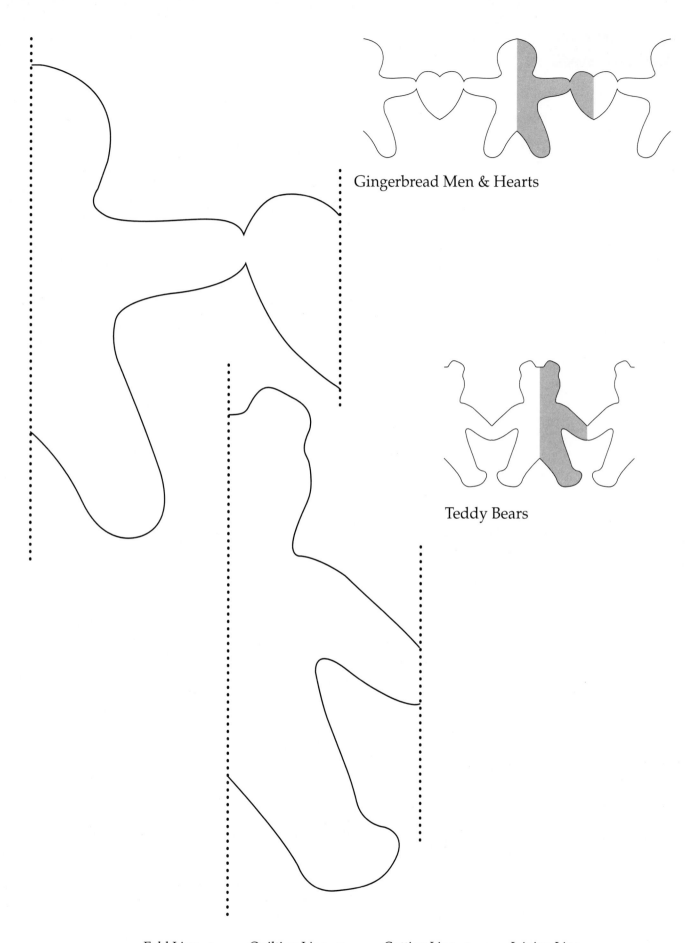

Gingerbread Men & Hearts

Teddy Bears

· · · · Fold Line • - - -Quilting Line • ——Cutting Line • -·-·Joining Line

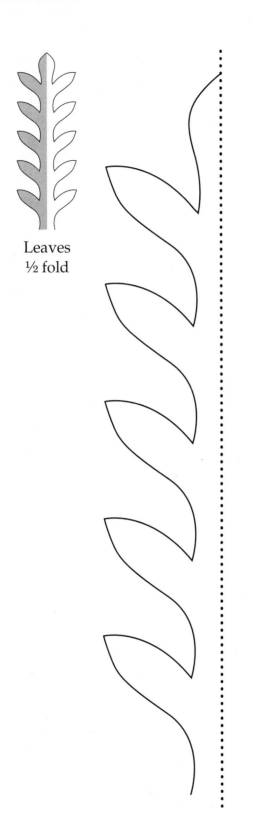

Leaves
½ fold

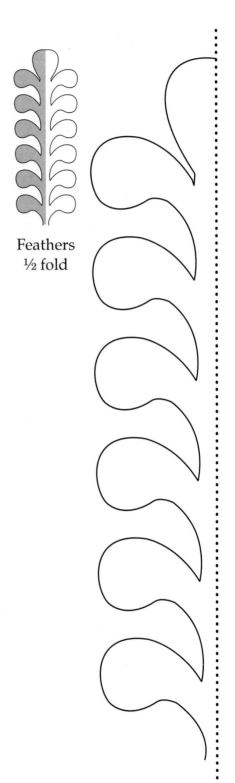

Feathers
½ fold

Reduce or enlarge as needed.

· · · · Fold Line   •   - - - Quilting Line   •   —— Cutting Line   •   -·-· Joining Line

QUILTING DESIGNS

Thistle
⅛ fold

Flower & Leaves

· · · · Fold Line • - - - Quilting Line • ——— Cutting Line • -·-· Joining Line

BIBLIOGRAPHY

Akana, Elizabeth. *Hawaiian Quilting, A Fine Art*, EA of Hawaii, Kailua, HI, 1981.

Allen, Gloria Seaman and Nancy Gibson Tuckhorn. *A Maryland Album: Quiltmaking Traditions~1634–1934*, Rutledge Hill Press, Nashville, TN, 1995.

Clark, Ricky. *Quilted Gardens: Floral Quilts of the Nineteenth Century*, Rutledge Hill Press, Nashville, TN, 1994.

Dewhurst, Kurt C. and Marsha MacDowell, eds. *To Honor and Comfort: Native Quilting Traditions*. Santa Fe, NM: Museum of New Mexico Press in collaboration with Michigan State University Museum, 1997.

Dunton, Dr. William Rush, Jr. *Old Quilts*, Baltimore, MD, 1946.

Fox, Sandi. *For Purpose and Pleasure: Quilting Together in Nineteenth-Century America*, Rutledge Hill Press, Nashville, TN, 1995.

_____. *Small Endearments: Nineteenth-Century Quilts for Children and Dolls*, Rutledge Hill Press, Nashville, TN, 1985, 1994.

Goldsborough, Jennifer. *Lavish Legacies: Baltimore Album and Related Quilts in the Collection of the Maryland Historical Society*, MHS, Baltimore, MD, 1994.

Guest, Carolyn. "Sheep Shear Cuttings: Paper Cutting in the Polish Style "(brochure), 459 Old Concord Rd., East St. Johnsbury, VT 05838.

Hammond, Joyce D. *Tifaifai and Quilts of Polynesia*, University of Hawaii Press, Honolulu, HI, 1986.

Jones, Stella M. *Hawaiian Quilts*, Daughters of Hawaii and Honolulu Academy of Arts and Mission Houses Museum, Honolulu, HI, 1973.

Kiracofe, Roderick with Mary Elizabeth Johnson. *The American Quilt: A History of Cloth and Comfort 1750–1950*, Clarkson Potter, NY, 1993.

Kolter, Jane Bentley. *Forget Me Not: A Gallery of Friendship and Album Quilts*, Sterling Publishing Co. Inc., NY, 1990.

Lasansky, Jeanette. *Pieced by Mother: Over 100 Years of Quiltmaking Traditions, Oral Traditions Project*, Lewisburg, PA, 1987.

Orlofsky, Patsy and Myron. *Quilts in America*, McGraw-Hill 1971, reprint Abbeville Press, Inc., NY, 1992.

Peto, Florence. *American Quilts and Coverlets*, Chanticleer Press, NY, 1949.

Rae, Janet. *The Quilts of the British Isles*, E.P. Dutton, NY, 1987.

Ramsey, Bets and Merikay Waldvogel. *The Quilts of Tennessee: Images of Domestic Life Prior to 1930*, Rutledge Hill Press, Nashville, TN, 1986.

Rich, Chris. *The Book of Papercutting*, Sterling Publishing Co. Inc., NY, 1994.

Root, Elizabeth. *Hawaiian Quilting*, Dover Publications, Inc., NY, 1989.

Roxanne International catalog, 3009 Peachwillow Lane, Walnut Creek, CA 94598.

Safford, Carleton L. and Robert Bishop. *America's Quilts and Coverlets*, E.P. Dutton, NY, 1980.

Sandstrom, Alan R. *Traditional Curing and Crop Fertility Rituals Among Otomi Indians of the Sierra de Puebla, Mexico: The Lopez Manuscripts*, Indiana University Publications, 1981.

Schlapfer-Geiser, Susanne. *Scherenschnitte: Designs and Techniques for Traditional Papercutting*, Paul Haupt Publishers, Berne, 1994. English translation, Lark Books, Asheville, NC, 1996.

Schorsch, Anita. *Plain & Fancy: Country Quilts of the Pennsylvania-Germans*, Sterling Publishing Co. Inc., NY, 1992.

Shaw, Robert. *Hawaiian Quilt Masterpieces*, Hugh Lauter Levin Assoc. Inc., 1996.

Valentine, Fawn with the West Virginia Heritage Quilt Search, Inc. *Echos from the Hills: West Virginia Quilts and Quiltmakers*, Davis & Elkins College, Elkins, WV, 1999.

Woodard, Thomas K. and Blanche Greenstein. *Classic Crib Quilts and How to Make Them*, Dover Publications, Inc., Mineola, NY, 1983.

ABOUT THE AUTHOR

Anita Shackelford is well known for her album quilts which combine original, personalized designs with nineteenth century dimensional appliqué techniques. Her first two books, *Three Dimensional Appliqué and Embroidery Embellishment: Techniques for Today's Album Quilt* and *Anita Shackelford: Surface Textures*, reflect her interest in dimensional appliqué, trapunto, and fine hand quilting. Anita enjoys working with a variety of styles and techniques in her quilts. With this book, she explores the exciting possibilities of creating original folded cutwork designs for appliqué.

An award-winning quiltmaker, with eleven Best of Show awards and many for workmanship, she is currently the only quiltmaker to have twice won the National Quilting Association's Mary Krickbaum award for excellence in hand quilting. Her work has been published in *American Quilter, American Patchwork & Quilting, Better Homes & Gardens' Fashion Ideas, McCall's Quilting, Quilter's Newsletter Magazine, Quilting Today, Quilt Craft, Quilting International, Traditional Quilter, Patchwork Quilt Tsushin, Americana* magazine, *Award Winning Quilts & Their Makers Vol. I*, and *The Quilt: Beauty in Fabric and Thread*. She has been making quilts since 1967 and teaching since 1980.

Anita is a member of the National Quilting Association and served for four years on the Board of Directors as membership chairman. She is a member of American Quilter's Society, The Appliqué Society, American Quilt Study Group, Baltimore Appliqué Society, and other local and regional guilds. She is a quilt judge, certified by NQA.

Anita lives in Bucyrus, Ohio, with her husband Richard. Their family also includes two daughters, Jennifer and Elisa, a son-in-law Scott and two grandchildren, Amber and Brandon. In addition to making her own quilts and writing about quiltmaking, Anita spends much of her time teaching and lecturing on her favorite subject — quilts.

Other Great Books by
ANITA SHACKELFORD

Learn award-winning techniques for appliqué, 3-D embellishment, and hand quilting in Anita Shackelford's series of books.

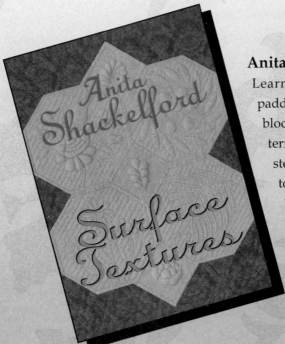

Anita Shackelford: Surface Textures

Learn how to add texture to your quilts by using cording, padding, stuffing, and background quilting. Twenty-five small blocks illustrate various techniques, complemented by a pattern section that includes two dozen 8" blocks. The step-by-step workbook and colorful gallery of quilts will inspire you to try each pattern.

136 pgs., 8½" x 11", HB (ISBN: 0-89145-890-5), #4829, **$24.95**

Three-Dimensional Appliqué and Embroidery Embellishment: Techniques for Today's Album Quilt

This comprehensive guide is sure to provide both the information and the inspiration you are seeking for developing your own traditional or contemporary album blocks. Included are 65 small blocks you can use as inspiration or as projects.

152 pgs., 9"x 12", HB (ISBN: 0-89145-819-0), #3788, **$24.95**

ORDER TOLL-FREE • 1-800-626-5420

American Quilter's Society

P. O. Box 3290 • Paducah, KY 42002-3290
FAX 502-898-8890 *http://www.AQSquilt.com*

Available at local quilt, fabric, and book stores, or order direct.

For a complete listing of AQS titles, write or call the American Quilter's Society.